THE BOOK OF ZEB-UN-NISSA
The Princess Sufi Poet 'Makhfi'

For a complete list of our publications

go to the back of this book

THE BOOK OF ZEB-UN-NISSA

The Princess Sufi Poet 'Makhfi'

Translation & Introduction

Paul Smith

NEW HUMANITY BOOKS
BOOK HEAVEN
Booksellers & Publishers

Copyright © Paul Smith 2012

NEW HUMANITY BOOKS

Book Heaven

(Booksellers & Publishers for over 40 years)

47 Main Road

Campbells Creek Victoria 3451

Australia

ISBN: 978-1507757734

www.newhumanitybooks.com

Poetry/Mysticism/Sufism/Indian Poetry/
Sufi Poetry/Women's Studies/ Mughal Poetry

Front Cover Painting of Princess Zeb-un-Nissa (Makhfi)
by Abanindranath Tagore

CONTENTS

The Life and Times and Poetry of Princess Zeb-un-Nissa...
Page 7

Sufis & Dervishes: Their Art & Use of Poetry... 33

The Poetic Forms in Makhfi's *Divan*... 57

Selected Bibliography... 69

Glossary... 71

Ruba'is... 77

Ghazals... 87

I fell into love's trap... yet, I'm free,
one of the dervish band;
and although my back's bent,
in the shadow of cypress... tall
I remain.

Life & Times & Poetry of Princess Zeb-un-Nissa

The Princess Zeb-un-Nissa (pen-name or *takhallus* 'Makhfi' meaning, 'veiled' or 'hidden') was the oldest daughter of the Mogul Emperor Aurangzeb of India, and was born in 1639. She came in direct descent from Genghiz Khan and Tamerlane. Her ancestors were famous not only for their cruelty and bravery and statesmanship but as patrons and inspirers of art, learning, and some of them possessed distinguished literary gifts. Babur's reminiscences are written in a fresh and delightful style and he wrote poetry both in Turkish and Persian, inventing a new style of verse. One of his sons Mirza Kamran was also a writer of Persian poetry. Although Akbar has given the world no writings of his own, tradition even says that he never found time to learn to write, yet he surrounded himself with a most cultured circle; and Abul Fazl his talented minister, constantly records in his letters Akbar's wise sayings and noble sentiments. Jehangir, like Babur, wrote his own memoirs and they are ranked high in Persian literature. Shah Jahan wrote some account of his court and of his travels and a record called the *Dastur-ul-Amal,* or Laws of Shah Jahan. Aurangzeb wrote books on Muslim law, and the collection of his letters called the *Ruqat Alamgiri,* is famous. Nor was this literary talent confined to the men's side of the house, Babur's daughter Gulbadan, wrote some history of her times and has left an interesting picture of Babur himself... and Zeb-un-Nissa's poetry testifies to her talent as a poet.

It is difficult to learn precisely the details of her life; they were not written in any detailed biography (until a recent one by Annie Krieger Krynicki, *Captive Princess: Zebunissa, Daughter of Emperor Aurangzeb,* Oxford, Karachi, 2005), for in her later days she incurred the wrath of her stern father and no court chronicler dared to speak of her.

Her mother was Dilrus Banu Begum, daughter of Shah Nawaz Khan. From her childhood she showed great intelligence and she received an education from an early age. At seven years old she was a *hafiz*... she knew the *Koran* by heart; and her father gave a great feast to celebrate the occasion. We read that the whole army was feasted in the great Maidan at Delhi, thirty thousand gold *mohurs* were given to the poor, and the public offices were closed for two days.

She was given as teacher a lady named Miyabai and learned Arabic in four years; she then studied mathematics and astronomy in which sciences she gained rapid proficiency. She began to write a commentary on the *Koran,* but this was stopped by her father. From her early youth she wrote poetry at first in

Arabic, but when an Arabian scholar saw her work he said: "Whoever has written this poem is Indian. The couplets are clever and wise, but the idiom is Indian although it is a miracle for a foreigner to know Arabic so well." This piqued her desire for perfection and from then on she wrote in Persian, her mother-tongue. She had as tutor a scholar called Shah Rustum Ghazi who encouraged and directed her literary tastes. She wrote at first in secret but he found copies of her poems among her exercise-books. He prophesised her future greatness and persuaded her father to send all over India and Persia and Kashmir to find poets and to invite them to come to Delhi to form a fitting circle for the princess. This was amazing as the fundamentalist Muslim Aurangzeb himself cared little for poetry and used to speak against poets. He had forbidden the works of Hafiz (her favourite) to be read in school by boys or in the palace by the women, but he made an exception in favour of Zeb-un-Nissa. When Zeb-un-Nissa was 21 years old, her father seized the throne from his father, Shah Jahan.

Among the poets and literary figures of her circle were Nasir Ali, Sayab Shamsh Wali Ullah (who was fascinated by her and composed poems praising her), Brahim, and Behraaz who was a great poet, and Saib Tabrizi Sharush. .Mullah Mohammed Ardebil translated a commentary on the *Koran* by Imam

Fakhruddin Razi from Arabic to Persian and in honour of her he gave her the title of *Zaib al Tafari* (worthy of praise). Mirza Khalil the scholar was also employed by her. The other great poet of Aurangzeb's time was Bedil (1644-1721), the great exponent of the 'Indian style' of *ghazal* (see my *Bedil: Selected Poems, New Humanity Books, 2012.*). He was also known to frequent the princess' gatherings.

Nasir Ali came from Sirhind and was famous for Sufi poetry, his pride and his poverty for he despised the protection of the great. Zeb-un-Nissa admired his poems and in a way he came to be regarded almost as her rival poet. Here are three of his *ruba'is…*

You, who an abundance of generosity are possessing,
you have young eyes… yet much patience are having.
The sighs of those who are suffering, do not ignore…
sharp as knives are slivers of an iron boat, now sinking.

All is fine in the place it should be, where it's right;
what's right you might think wrong… at first sight.
A shadow on a night moon lights, might look ugly,
on a day sun's light shines brightly… it looks right!

After we become men of the Faith, our faithlessness stays:
mischievous sweetheart quarrels after another 'sorry' says.
We passed away, infidel self in us didn't: what to do next?
Adam became one with the dust, but... Satan, alive stays.

Her coterie used to engage in a poetical tournament, a kind of war of wits. One would propose a line, sometimes it would be a question; another would answer it or contradict it or qualify it or expand it, by a line or lines in the same metre, rhyming with the original line. This is called *musha'irah* and in this quick repartee Zeb-un-Nissa excelled.

Aurangzeb grew weary of her fame and renown throughout the land and decided to teach her a lesson. He invited Nasir Ali to his court for a poetry contest with his daughter. Ali was one of the most ardent suitors of Zeb-un-Nissa and one of the best poets in the land. The challenge was that Nasir Ali would recite the first line of a couplet and she would have to complete it within three days, if she failed she would have to renounce her poetry forever. Aurangzeb had instructed Nasir Ali to compose such a difficult line that no one in the kingdom could complete it. He went ahead and composed the following: "Rare it is to find a black and white pearl." When she heard this she was distressed, no one seemed to able to help her... where would one find a black and white pearl, let alone compose a couplet on it?

She felt humiliated and crushed, a poet as accomplished as her not being able to complete one line. At the end of three days and still no line. She preferred to die than give up her poetry, so she prepared for her last moments by calling her best friend, her beautiful Hindu servant friend Imami who was also a poet (some say her lover) to her quarters. As Zeb-un-Nissa prepared to eat her own diamond ring her beautiful friend clung to her and wept profuse tears of distress. As she wept Zeb-un-Nissa began to smile and clasped to her breast and exclaimed, "Weep no more my dear one... for I've found the second line of the couplet. She summoned Aurangzeb immediately to her palace and he came rushing, expecting to see her defeated and depressed. "I have your line, your Majesty," she said. Then she recited, "Rare it is to find a black and white pearl," and then, "Except a mingled tear of a beautiful dark girl!"

She had been betrothed by the wish of Shah Jahan her grandfather, to Suleiuian Shikoh, who was her cousin and son of her uncle Dara Shikoh. He was the oldest son of Emperor Shah Jahan and was known to be a loving husband, a good son and loving father. He was a fine poet, his poems having the influence of Sufism to which he was dedicated. He used 'Qadiri' as his *takhallus* or pen-name. His *Divan* of *ghazals*, *ruba'is* and *qasidas* in Persian was not the only work he left behind, his prose works on Sufism and mysticism are popular in India even today. His *Majma al-Bahrain* or *The Mingling of the Two Oceans* is an explanation of the mystical sameness of Sufism and Vedanta. He also translated the *Upanishads* into Persian.

Prince Dara Shikoh

He had a great breath of vision and was respected by many of the Sufi Masters of the time such as Shaikh Muhibbullah Allabadi, Miyan Mir and Mulla Badakhshi and the 'naked' Sufi poet Sarmad. He was greatly loved by Zeb-un-Nissa. After he was defeated after leading an uprising against his cruel, fundamentalist brother, he was brutally killed on the 21st of August 1659. Here are examples of some of his *ruba'is*...

We have not seen an atom separate from the sun...
and every drop of water has come from the ocean.
What is the name that one should call the Truth?
Each name in existence from one of His does come.

God's Unity is found in silence and meditation,
the Unity disappears when one's in a discussion.
Duality is created when you say, "God is One!"
When you proclaim it, God's Unity is like none!

To hurt my feelings you called me an unbeliever,
when I think about it... of it, I can't be a denier!
I can't find difference between higher and lower:
in all seventy-two sects of Islam, I'm a believer!

You want to be in circle of who are illuminated?
Well, stop all talk, and be in that state, instead!
By repeating 'God is One' you can't be the One,
like tongue can't taste sugar by having it uttered.

Separated from You, anxiety I have been suffering,
when being with You my consciousness I was losing.
Now, upon this soul of mine a blessing has dawned
and has become my lot... in body and mind, staying!

Unless you taste death your name can't become immortal,
unless you have a slave you cannot become a master at all.
The Truth was revealed because we had been created...
if we hadn't been created, God wouldn't be known, to recall.

Adam... mankind's father, Satan disowned, didn't he?
Hallaj said, "I am the Truth" and got killed, didn't he?
Really, it's the evil and malicious spirit of this priest...
every saint and every prophet he tormented, didn't he?

For one who is spiritual, death has no sting;
heart that's awake doesn't fear not sleeping.

It matters, if your soul abandons your body?
When skin gets old, a snake it off is casting.

The mystics keep going into a new state of ecstasy:
they are leaders of religion not followers... you see?
Lions are only eating what they have preyed upon...
what's left out in the sun the fox eats, unthinkingly.

The true mystic will enlighten your heart and your soul,
make a garden from thorns pulled from your foot's sole!
The Perfect One will purge all defects from each one...
one burning candle will a thousand light... make whole.

Two of his *ghazals*...

Look wherever you can, look and that all is God see...
God's face is always available, face to face, believe me.
Whatever you see except that One is your imagination,
all things other than that One are a mirage, not reality.
God's existence could be likened to an infinite ocean...
we're like bubbles and waves in its water flowing freely.
Although I don't think of myself as separate from God,
I still am not considering that I am God the Almighty!

*Whatever the relationship the drop has with the ocean,
in my belief that is the truth, nothing beyond it can be!
We have never seen an atom that from Sun is separate,
and… every drop of water is in essence the endless Sea.
Qadiri, what name is it that one should call the Truth?
Each name in this existence is one of God's… obviously.*

*Being a king's easy, try going and discovering poverty:
why would a drop be a pearl, when it the ocean can be?
Hands that with gold are soiled, they start stinking…
soul that's soiled with gold's an awful thing, honestly.
Every day and night. you are hearing of others dying…
you'll also die, the way you act is strange… stupidity!
The more that the traveler is without useless baggage
the less that traveler is feeling worried of the journey!
You also, in this old world are a traveler, this is true:
if you are one who is awake, take this as a certainty!
Make sure that you send away love of self from you;
because, it burden like arrogance and conceit will be.
For as long as you are living in this world, Qadri is
now giving you this warning: be an individual, free!*

Aurangzeb who hated and feared Dara, was unwilling that the marriage should take place and caused the young prince to be poisoned.

Aurangzeb reading the Koran.

Aurangzeb was a conservative Sunni and once in power, became increasingly severe in his requirements for the observance of his interpretations of Islamic law. However, his eldest sister Jahanra was a close friend and her brother Dara a Sufi who gave less emphasis to religious ritual and more to a personal devotion to God. Perhaps through the influence of her aunt and uncle, Zeb-un-Nissa eventually also chose the inner path of devotion. The Sufis held only a marginal place in Aurangzeb's society but unless they allied themselves with Aurangzeb's opponents, they were tolerated.

She had many other suitors for her hand but she demanded that she should see the princes and test their attainments before a match was arranged. One of those who wished to marry her was Mirza Farukh, son of Shah Abbas II of Iran; she wrote to him to come to Delhi so that she might see what he was like. The record remains of how he came with a splendid retinue and was feasted by her in a pleasure-house in her garden while she waited on him with her veil upon her face. He asked for a certain sweetmeat in words which by a play of language also meant a kiss, and Zeb-un-Nissa, affronted, said, "Ask for what you want from our kitchen." She told her father that in spite of the prince's beauty and rank, his bearing did not please her and she refused the marriage. Mirza Farukh however sent her this verse:

"I am determined never to leave this temple: here will I bow my head, here will I serve and here alone is happiness." Zeb-un-Nissa answered: "How light you make of this game of love, O child. You know nothing of the fever of longing and the fire of separation and the burning flame of love." And so he returned to Persia without her.

She was not attached to her own beauty as the following famous story tells. Once, Aurangazeb gave her a beautiful mirror as a birthday gift. Zeb-un-Nissa loved the mirror very much. One day her maid was holding the mirror to her while Zeb-un-Nissa was combing her hair after her bath. The mirror just slipped from the hand of the maid and broke into pieces. The maid was mortally afraid. She knew that the mirror was a precious gift, given to the princess and how much she loved it. The maid was prepared to accept any punishment her princess may give her. She fell at her feet. But Zeb-un-Nissa very calmly said with a smile: "Get up. I am glad the instrument of flattery is broken. Why worry over the broken mirror? Even this body to which all these articles are catering is liable to damage and to destruction."

She enjoyed a great deal of liberty in the palace: she wrote to many learned men of her time and held discussions with them. She was a great favourite with her uncle Dara Shikoh, who was a scholar, a poet, open-minded and enlightened. To him she modestly attributed her verses when first she began to write and many of the *ghazals* in the *Divan* of Dara Shikoh are really by her. She came out in the court and helped in her father's councils, but always with the veil upon her face. Perhaps she liked the metaphor of the face hidden till the day when the Divine Beloved should come; perhaps life behind carved lattices had a charm for her: for her pen-name she took Makhfi, the hidden one. Once Nasir Ali said this verse: "O envy of the moon, lift up your veil and let me enjoy the wonder of your beauty." She answered with…

I will not lift my veil: if I did… who knows,
the nightingale might then forget the rose…
Hindu worshipper adoring Lakshmi's grace
might turn, forsaking her… to see my face.
Think how in the rose hidden as in a bower
her fragrant soul is, none can see it, ever…
so me the world can see only in my poetry:
I will not lift the veil… me you will not see.

She was deeply religious, but she was a Sufi and did not share her father's cold and narrow orthodoxy. One day she was talking in the garden and moved by the beauty of the world around her, exclaimed, "Four things are necessary to make me happy... wine and flowers and a running stream and the face of Beloved." Again and again she recited the couplet; suddenly she noticed Aurangzeb on a marble platform under a tree close by, wrapt in meditation. She was seized with fear thinking he might have heard her words; but, as he had not noticed her she went on chanting as before, but with the second line changed to... "Four things are necessary for happiness: prayers, fasting, tears and repentance!"

She belonged like her father, to the Sunni sect of Muslims and was well educated in controversial religious points. One of Aurangzeb's sons Muhammad Ma'uzarn, was a Shi'a, and when sectarian disputes took place in the court the princess was often asked to settle them. Her decision in one dispute is famous for it was copied and sent to Iran and Turan, and many princesses are said to have been converted to the Sunni faith because of it. Much of her personal allowance of four *lakhs* a year she spent in encouraging men of letters, in providing for widows and orphans and in sending every year some pilgrims to Mecca and Medina.

She had built numerous astronomical observatories, schools and *sarais*. She collected a fine library and employed skilled calligraphers to copy rare and valuable books and translators to translate from the Arabic and Sanscrit into Persian important manuscripts for her… and as paper from Kashmir and Kashmiri scribes were famous for their excellence she had a scriptorium also in that province, where work went on constantly. Her personal interest in the work was great and every morning she went over the copies that had arrived on the previous day. She had contemporary fame as a poet and literary men used to send their works for her approval or criticism and she rewarded them according to their merits.

In personal appearance she is described as being tall and slim, her face round and fair in colour, with two moles or beauty-spots on her left cheek. Her eyes and abundant hair were very black and she had thin lips and small teeth. In Lahore Museum is a painted portrait of the time which corresponds to this description (see the cover of *Captive Princess*). She did not use *missia* for blackening between the teeth, nor antimony for darkening her eyelashes, even though this was the fashion of her time. Her voice was so beautiful that when she read the *Koran* she moved those listening to tears. In dress she was simple and austere; in later life she always wore white and her only ornament was a string of pearls around her neck. She is said to have invented a woman's garment, the *angya kurti,* a modification to suit Indian conditions of the dress of the women of Turkestan. It is now worn all over India. She was humble, courteous, patient and philosophic in enduring troubles; no one, it is said, ever saw her with a wrinkled forehead. Zeb-un-Nissa was skilled in the use of arms and several times took part in war.

In the beginning of 1662 Aurangzeb was taken ill and his physicians prescribed a change of air so he took his family and court with him to Lahore. At that time Akil Khan, the son of his prime-minister, was governor of that city. He was famous for being handsome and courageous and was also a poet. He had heard of Zeb-un-Nissa and knew her poems and was anxious to meet her. On the pretence of guarding the city he used to ride around the walls of the palace in the hope of catching a glimpse of her. One day he was fortunate; he saw her on the balcony at dawn dressed in a robe of *gulnar*, the colour of the flower of the pomegranate. He called out, "A vision in red on the balcony of the palace does appear." She heard and answered, completing the couplet: "Supplications nor force nor gold can ever win her."

She liked Lahore as a residence and was laying out a garden there: one day Akil Khan heard that she had gone with her companions to see a marble pavilion which was being built in its grounds. He disguised himself as a mason and carrying a mortar-board, managed to pass the guards and enter. She was playing *chausar* with some of her girlfriends and he, passing near, remarked: "In my longing for you, I've become like the dust, around the earth wandering." She understood and answered immediately: "Even if you had become like the wind, you should not a lock of my hair be touching." They met again and again, but a rumour reached the ears of Aurangzeb who was at Delhi and he rushed back to Lahore. He wished to hush up the matter by hurrying her into marriage at once. Zeb-un-Nissa demanded freedom of choice and asked that portraits of her suitors should be sent to her; and naturally she chose Akil Khan's. Aurangzeb sent for him; but a disappointed rival had written to her favourite: "It is no child's play to be the lover of a daughter of a king. Aurangzeb knows your doings; as soon as you come to Delhi, you will reap the fruit of your love." Akil Khan thought the emperor planned to kill him as he had her cousin years before. So, alas for poor Zeb-un-Nissa… at the critical moment her lover proved a coward; he declined the marriage and wrote to the king resigning his service. Zeb-un-Nissa was scornful and disappointed and wrote: "I hear that Akil Khan has left off paying homage to me"… the words might also mean, "has resigned service"… "on account of some foolishness." He answered, also in verse, "Why should a wise man do that which be knows he will regret?" (Akil also means a wise man). But, he came secretly to Delhi to see her again, perhaps regretting his fears. Again they met in her garden; the emperor was told and came unexpectedly, and Zeb-un-Nissa could think of no hiding-place for her lover but a *deg*... a large cooking-vessel. The emperor asked, "What is in the *deg*?" and she answered, "Only water to be heated." "Put it on the fire, then," he ordered; and it was done. Zeb-un-Nissa at that moment thought more of her reputation than of her lover and came near the *deg* and whispered: "Keep silence if you are my true lover, for the sake of my honour." One of her couplets says, "What is the fate of a lover? It is to be sacrificed for the world's pleasure." One wonders if when composing this she thought of Akil Khan's sacrifice of his life.

In 1681, when Zeb-un-Nissa was 44 years old the younger of her two brothers Akbar rebelled against his father and proclaimed himself emperor. The rebellion lasted only a month; Akbar fled the country but continued to be troublesome. Zeb-un-Nissa had some communication with her exiled brother and was accused by Aurangzeb of being the rebel's ally; for this she was imprisoned in the Delhi fortress of Salimargh and disappeared from the official record; others say she was imprisoned because of her sympathy with the Mahratta chieftain and Spiritual Master Shivaji. There she spent twenty long years, and there she wrote much bitter poetry...

For as long as these chains to my feet are clinging,
friends are foes... relations strangers are becoming.
I am still being anxious to keep the honour of my
name when friends' to disgrace me keep on trying?
Do not be looking for relief from the prison of grief,
for not politically prudent for one, is our releasing.
From the grave of Majnun the voice comes to me:
"O Layla, love's victim, even here has no resting!"
I have passed all of my life and have only sorrow,
and repentance and unfulfilled tears... of longing!
O Makhfi, there is no hope of release for you to be
having 'til the Day of Judgment is finally arriving.

When her memory was becoming dim in the hearts of her friends, Nasir Ali alone thought of her and wrote a poem to her saying that now the world could not delight in her presence and he himself had to go about the earth unhappy, having no one but himself to appreciate his poetry. But she sent no answering word, perhaps never receiving it. He died on March 29, 1697

Many couplets she wrote in prison are very melancholic, telling of the faithlessness of the times...

Makhfi, why should you complain of friends or enemies?
Fate has frowned upon you, from the beginning of time.

Let no one know the secrets of your love…
on the way of love, O Makhfi, walk alone.
Tell him you don't desire his comradeship
even if Jesus seeks to be your companion.

O useless arms, you never held that lost Beloved;
better to be broken than eternally empty and cold.
O worthless eyes, that lost Beloved you didn't see
all these years, better blind than by tears dimmed!
O foolish things, not to bring Beloved home to me:
friends of my youth have left, taken their own road.
O fading rose, born hidden and dying in dust like
heart's bloom, never on His turban to be displayed.

Zeb-un-Nissa died in 1701 after seven days illness still imprisoned in Shahjahanabad (old Delhi) while Aurangzeb was on a trip to the Deccan. Her tomb was in the garden of 'Thirty thousand trees', outside of the Kabuli Gate. But when the railway line was laid out at Delhi her tomb was shifted to Akbar's mausoleum at Sikandara, Agra.

The garden which she laid out in Lahore itself and which was called the Chauburgi, or four-towered, can still be traced by portions of the walls and gates remaining. Three of the turrets over the archway still stand, ornamented with tiles in patterns of cypress-trees and growing flowers, and the gateways have inscriptions in Arabic and Persian. One of these tells that she presented the garden to her old instructress Miyabai.

In 1724, what could be found of her scattered writings were collected under the name of the *Divan-i-Makhfi*, literally... the Book of the Hidden One. It contained four hundred and twenty-one *ghazals* and several *ruba'is*. In 1730 other *ghazals* were added. Many manuscript copies were made in both India and Persia; some beautifully illuminated examples are known and preserved.

The *Divan of Makhfi* shares the characteristics of other Sufi poetry... the worship of God under the form of the Beloved, who is adorable but tyrannical, who reduces the lover to abject despair, but at last bestows on the lover a gleam of hope when at the point of depth. The Beloved is the Hunter of the Soul, chasing it like a deer through the jungle of the world. The lover is the madman who for his love is scorned and mocked by the unsympathetic world. The personified Power of Evil, the Enemy, lurks at the devotee's elbow, ready to distract the lover from the contemplation of God.

She was evidently acquainted not only with the theories of Sufism but with the practices of the *fakirs* as well. But the poems of Zeb-un-Nissa, in addition to what they share with other Sufi poetry, have a special Indian flavour of their own. She inherited the tradition of the unification of religions and knew not only Islam but Hinduism and Zoroastrianism also. Her special triumph consists in that she weaves together the religious traditions and harmonizes them with Sufi practices. In some of her poems she hails the sun as the symbol of deity. Constantly she speaks of the mosque and the temple together or antithetically in saying that God is equally in both or too great to be worshipped in either. Sometimes she even combines the Hindu and Muslim ideas. The major influences on her are said to have been the poetry of Hafiz and that of the Hindu poetess/saint and devotee of Krishna, Mira Bai.

The glorification or adoration of the *pir*, or Spiritual Master is also shown in her poems. He is the intermediary between God and man (see glossary).

In addition to her poetic book or collection of poems, called a *Divan*, which contains approximately 5,000 couplets, she has also written the following books: *Monis-ul-Roh, Zeb-ul Monsha'at and Zeb-ul-Tafasir*. In *Maghzan-ul Ghara'eb*, the author writes that the *Divan* of Zeb-un-Nissa contained 15,000 couplets. Her *Divan* was printed in Delhi in 1929 and in Tehran in 2001. Its manuscripts are in the National Library of Paris,

Library of the British Museum, Library of Tübingen University in Germany and in the Mota Library in India.

The *Divan-i-Makhfi* is widely read in India and is highly esteemed. Its poetry is chanted in the ecstatic concourses which meet at festivals at the tombs of celebrated saints; so that, although her tomb has been spoiled of the splendour which befitted the resting-place of a Mogul princess she has the immortality her father perhaps would have desired. In one of her couplets she says: "I am the daughter of a king, but I have taken the path of renunciation and this is my glory, as my name Zeb-un-Nissa, being interpreted... means that I am the glory of womankind!"

Sufis & Dervishes: Their Art and Use of Poetry

It has been said that Adam was the first Sufi and Perfect Master *(Qutub)* and that he was also the first poet as he named everything and so through his 'Adamic Alphabet' (see the *Hebraic Tongue Restored* listed below) all languages were born and so... all poetry. Two of Arabia's most highly regarded scholars of the poetic form also claim he was the father of the poetic form of the *ghazal*... the form most used by Sufi and Dervish poets up to the present day).

Sufism is said by many Masters and authors to have always existed since Adam as the esoteric side of each faith that has begun by an appearance of that original Perfect Master coming back as the Rasool, Prophet, Messiah, Avatar, Buddha, etc., whatever that Divine One is called.

Many Perfect Masters *(Qutubs)* were poets and many were not. Many came after the appearance of the Prophet Mohammed and many came before him. But, Sufis and Dervishes were called by those names after he passed from this world. The first 'Sufi' or 'Dervish' is probably Mohammed's son-in-law Hazrat Ali who composed one of the first *ghazals* ever recorded that essentially sums up the meaning of Sufism and Dervishness...

You do not know it, but in you is the remedy;
you cause the sickness, but this you don't see.
You are but a small form... this, you assume:
but you're larger than any universe, in reality.
You are the book that of any fallacies is clear,
in you are all letters spelling out, the mystery.
You are the Being, you're the very Being... It:
you contain That, which contained cannot be!

I have used both the terms 'Sufi' and 'Dervish' in this book because Samad was called a 'Sufi' by others but saw himself more as a 'Dervish' for... during the time that he was alive, many 'Sufis' had become corrupt and were following false masters. Hafiz likewise always called himself a Dervish and often when mentioning Sufis in his poetry it was usually to criticize them. During his lifetime in Shiraz there was an extremist Sufi Order led by a false master and Shaikh Ali Kolah who sided with various dictators and subjected the people to a very vicious brand of fundamentalism. By the 13th century many Sufi Orders had become corrupt and full of various dogmas, useless rituals and power hungry and hypocritical shaikhs and false masters. Those who called themselves 'Dervishes' then really meant 'true Sufis'.

The first Sufi and Dervish poets composed in Arabic even though some of them, including the famous and infamous Sufi martyr Mansur al-Hallaj, were originally from Persia... he was from near Shiraz. From the 10th to the 17th century the vast majority of Sufi and Dervish and other poets in the region composed in Persian, a few in the new languages of Turkish and Urdu and some like Kabir in Hindi; after that... the languages most used by the most conscious and influential poets were Urdu, Punjabi and Sindhi, as the stream of God-consciousness moved originally from Arabia and Egypt to Iraq and Syria then into Iran and Afghanistan and Turkey and finally into the Indian Sub-Continent.

To follow this golden thread of Spiritual Poetry one must follow the true Spiritual Hierarchy of real Saints and God-realized Souls... Perfect Masters, their lives and stories are to be found in the many books listed below and in many others.

What is the essential belief and philosophy of the Sufi and Dervish Masters and Poets? To put it as simply as possibly... The Love of God, the belief in God in human form, the love and respect for all of God's Creation and to try to not hurt anyone or thing. And of course a belief in Truth, Love and Beauty as the greatest of the Divine Attributes. A belief similar, if not the same as the Christian Mystics and Vedantists and believers in the inner way of most religions.

Hazrat Inayat Khan says in his essay on Sufi Poetry: "There is a saying that a poet is a prophet, and this saying has a great significance and a hidden meaning. There is no doubt that though poetry is not necessarily prophecy, prophecy is born in poetry. If one were to say that poetry is a body which is adopted by the spirit of prophecy, it would not be wrong. Wagner has said that noise is not necessarily music, and the same thing can be said in connection with poetry: that a verse written in rhyme and metre is not necessarily true poetry. Poetry is an art, a music expressed in the beauty and harmony of words. No doubt much of the poetry one reads is meant either as a pastime or for amusement, but real poetry comes from the dancing of the soul. And no one can make the soul dance unless the soul itself is inclined to dance. Also, no soul can dance which is not alive.

In the Bible it is said that no one will enter the kingdom of God whose soul is not born again, and being born means being alive. It is not only a happy disposition or an external inclination to merriment and pleasure that is the sign of a living soul; for external joy and amusement may come simply through the external being of man, although even in this outer joy and happiness there is a glimpse of the inner joy and happiness which is the sign of the soul having been born again. What makes it alive? It makes itself alive when it strikes its depths instead of reaching outward. The soul, after coming up against the iron wall of this life of falsehood, turns back within itself, it encounters itself, and this is how it becomes living.

In order to make this idea more clear I should like to take as an example a man who goes out into the world; a man with thought, with feeling, with energy, with desire, with ambition, with enthusiasm to live and work in life. And because of the actual nature of life, his experience will make him feel constantly up against an iron wall in whatever direction he strikes out. And the nature of man is such that when he meets with an obstacle then he struggles; he lives in the outer life, and he goes on struggling. He does not know any other part of life, for he lives only on the surface. But then there is another man who is sensitive because he has a sympathetic and tender heart, and every blow coming from the outer world, instead of making him want to hit back outwardly, makes him want to strike at himself inwardly. And the consequence of this is that his soul, which after being born on this earth seems to be living but in reality is in a grave, becomes awakened by that action; and when once the soul is awakened in this way it expresses itself outwardly, whether in music, in art, in poetry, in action, or in whatever way it wishes to express itself.

In this way a poet is born. There are two signs which reveal the poet: one sign is imagination, the other is feeling, and both are essential on the spiritual path. A man, however learned and good, who yet lacks these two qualities, can never arrive at a satisfactory result, especially on the spiritual path.

The sacred scriptures of all ages, whether of the Hindus or the Parsis, the race of Ben Israel or of others, were all given in poetry or in poetic prose. No spiritual person however great, however pious and spiritually advanced, has ever been able to give a scripture to the world unless he was blessed with the gift of poetry. One may ask if this would still be possible nowadays, when sentiment takes second place in life's affairs and people wish everything to be expressed plainly, 'cut and dried' as the saying is, and when one has become so accustomed to having everything, especially in science, explained in clear words. But it must be understood that facts about the names and forms of this world may be scientifically explained in plain words, but when one wishes to interpret the sensation one gets when looking at life, it cannot be explained except in the way that the prophets did in poetry. No one has ever explained nor can anyone ever explain the truth in words. Language exists only for the convenience of everyday affairs; the deepest sentiments cannot be explained in words. The message that the prophets have given to the world at different times is an interpretation in their own words of the idea of life that they have received.

Inspiration begins in poetry and culminates in prophecy. One can picture the poet as a soul which has so to speak risen from its grave and is beginning to make graceful movements; but when the same soul begins to move and to dance in all directions and to touch heaven and earth in its dance, expressing all the beauty it sees -- that is prophecy. The poet when he is developed reads the mind of the universe, although it very often happens that the poet himself does not know the real meaning of what he has said. Very often one finds that a poet has said something, and after many years there comes a moment when he realizes the true meaning of what he said. And this shows that behind all these different activities the divine Spirit is hidden, and the divine Spirit often manifests through an individual without his realizing that it is divine.

In the East the prophet is called *Payghambar*, which means the Messenger, the one who carries somebody's word to someone else. In reality every individual in this world is the medium of an impulse which is hidden behind him, and that impulse he gives out, mostly without knowing it. This is not only so with living beings, but one can see it even in objects; for every object has its purpose, and by fulfilling its purpose that object is fulfilling the scheme of nature. Therefore whatever be the line or activity of a man, whether it is business or science or music or art or poetry, he is a medium in some way or other. There are mediums of living beings, there are mediums of those who have passed to the other side, and there are mediums that represent their country, their nation, their race. Every individual is acting in his own way as a medium.

When the prophet or the poet dives deep into himself he touches that perfection which is the source and goal of all beings. And as an electric wire connected with a battery receives the force or energy of the battery, so the poet who has touched the innermost depths of his being has touched the perfect God, and from there he derives that wisdom, that beauty, and that power which belong to the perfect Self of God. There is no doubt that in all things there is the real and the false and there is the raw and the ripe. Poetry comes from the tendency to contemplation. A man with imagination cannot retain the imagination, cannot mould it, cannot build it up unless he has this contemplative tendency within him. The more one contemplates the more one is able to conceive of what one receives. Not only this, but after contemplation a person is able to realize a certain idea more clearly than if that idea had only passed through his mind.

The process of contemplation is like the work of the camera: when the camera is put before a certain object and has been properly focused, then only that object is received by the camera. And therefore when an object before one is limited, then one can see that object more clearly. What constitutes the appeal of the poet is that he tells his readers of something he has seen behind these generally recognized ideas. The prophet goes still further. He not only contemplates one idea, but he can contemplate on any idea: There comes a time in the life of the prophet or of anyone who contemplates, when whatever object he casts his glance upon opens up and reveals to him what it has in its heart. In the history of the world we see that besides their great imagination, their great dreams, their ecstasy and their joy in the divine life, the prophets have often been great reformers, scientists, medical men or even statesmen.

This in itself shows their balance; it shows that theirs is not a one-sided development; they do not merely become dreamers or go into trances, but both sides of their personality are equally development. It is an example of God in man that the prophets manifest. We can see this in the life of Joseph: we are told that he was so innocent, so simple that he went with his brothers, yielding to them, and that this led to his betrayal. In his relationship with Zuleikha we see the human being, the tendency to beauty. And at the same time there is the question he continually asks: What am I doing? What shall I do? Later in his life we see him as one who knows the secret of dreams, as the mystic who interprets the dream of the king. And still later in his life we see that he became a minister, with the administration of the country in his hands, able to carry out the work of the state.

Spirituality has become far removed from material life, and so God is far removed from humanity. Therefore one cannot any more conceive of God speaking through a man, through someone like oneself even a religious man who reads the Bible every day will have great difficulty in understanding the verse, 'Be ye perfect, even as your Father in heaven is perfect.' The Sufi message and its mission are to bring this truth to the consciousness of the world: that man can dive so deep within himself that he can touch the depths where he is united with the whole of life, with all souls, and that he can derive from that source harmony, beauty, peace, and power.

Sufi poetic imagery stands by itself, distinct and peculiar in its character. It is both admired and criticized for its peculiarity. Why it is different from the expressions of other poets born in various countries, is because of its Persian origin and the particular qualities of Persia - the fine climate, the ancient traditions, its being the place where, it is said, wine was tasted for the first time; a land of luxury, a land of beauty, a land of art and imagination. It was natural that with Persian thinkers of all periods, who thought deeply on life, its nature and character, their expressions should become subtle, artistic, fine, and picturesque. In short, it is the dancing of the soul. In all other living beings, the soul is lying asleep, but when once the soul has awakened, called by beauty, it leaps up dancing, and its every movement makes a picture, whether in writing, poetry, music or whatever it may be. A dancing soul will always express the most subtle and intricate harmonies in the realm of music or poetry.

When we read the works of Hafiz and of many other Sufi poets, we shall find that they are full of the same imagery and this is partly because that was the time of Islam. The mission of Islam had a particular object in view, and in order to attain that object it had strict rules about life. A free-thinker had difficulty in expressing his thoughts without being accused of having done a great wrong towards the religion and the State. And these free- thinkers of Persia, with their dancing soul and continual enthusiasm, began to express their soul in this particular imagery, using words such as 'the beloved', 'wine', 'wine-press', and 'tavern'. And this poetry became so popular that not only the wise derived benefit from it, but also the simple ones enjoyed the beauty of its wonderful expressions which make an immediate appeal to every soul. There is no doubt that the souls which were already awakened and those on the point of awakening were inspired by these poems. Souls which were opening their eyes after the deep slumber of many years began to rise up and dance; as Hafiz says, 'If those pious ones of long robes listen to my verse, my song, they will immediately begin to get up and dance'. And then he says at the end of the poem, 'Forgive me, O pious ones, for I am drunk just now!'

This concept of drinking is used in various connections and conveys many different meanings. In the first place, imagine that there is a magic tavern where there are many different kinds of wine. Each wine has a different effect upon the person who drinks it. One drinks a wine which makes him light-hearted, frivolous, humorous; another drinks a wine which makes him sympathetic, kind, tender, gentle. Someone else drinks one which makes him bewildered at everything he sees. Another drinks and finds his way into the ditch. One becomes angry after drinking while another becomes passionate. One drinks and is drowned in despair. Another drinks and begins to feel loving and affectionate; yet another drinks a wine that makes him discouraged with everything. Imagine how interested we should all be to see that tavern! In point of fact we live in that tavern and we see it every day; only, we do not take proper notice of it.

Once I saw a Madzub, (one who is absorbed in a plane of involving consciousness) a man who pretends to be insane, who though living in the world does not wish to be of the world, standing in the street of a large city, laughing. I stood there, feeling curious to know what made him laugh at that moment. And I understood that it was the sight of so many drunken men, each one having had his particular wine.

It is most amusing when we look at it in this way. There is not one single being on earth who does not drink wine; only, the wine of one is different from the wine of the other. A man does not only drink during the day but the whole night long, and he awakens in the morning intoxicated by whatever wine he has been drinking. He awakens with fear or with anger, he awakens with joy, or with love and affection; and the moment he awakens from sleep he shows what wine he has been drinking.

One might ask why the great Sufi teachers have taken such a great interest in the particular imagery of these poets. The reason is that they found the solution to the problem of life by looking upon the world as a tavern, with many wines and each person drinking a different one. They discovered the alchemy, the chemical process, by which to change the wine that a person drinks, and give him another wine to see how this works. The work of the Sufi teacher with his pupil is of that kind. He first finds out which blend of wine his *mureed* (disciple) drinks, and then he finds out which blend be must have.

But, one will ask, is there then no place for soberness in life? There is, but when that soberness is properly interpreted, one sees that it too is wine. Amir (Khusraw), the Hindustani poet, has expressed it in verse, 'The eyes of the sober one spoke to the eyes of the drunken one: "You have no place here, for your intoxication is different from mine."' The awakened person seems to be asleep to the sleeping one, and so the one who has become sober also appears to be still drunk; for the condition of life is such that no one appears to be sober. It is this soberness which is called *Nirvana* by Buddhists and *Mukti* by Hindus. But if I were asked if it is then desirable for me to be sober, my reply would be, no. What is desirable is for us to know whet soberness is, and after knowing what soberness is, then to take any wine we may choose. The tavern is there; wines are there. There are two men: one who is the master of wine, the other who is the slave of wine; the first drinks wine, but wine drinks up the other. The one whom wine drinks up is mortal; he who drinks wine becomes immortal. What is the love of God? What is divine knowledge? Is it not a wine? Its experience is different, its intoxication is different, for there is ordinary wine and there is most costly champagne. The difference is in the wine.

In the imagery of the Sufi poets this tavern (winehouse) is the world, and the Saki (Winebringer) is God. In whatever form the wine-giver comes and gives a wine, it is God who comes. In this way, by recognizing the Saki, the wine-giver, in all forms, the Sufi worships God;. for he recognizes Him in friend and foe as the wine-giver. And wine is that influence which we receive *from* life, an harmonious influence or a depressing influence, a beautiful influence or one that lacks beauty. When we have given in to it then we become drunk, then we become addicted to it, then we are under its influence; but when we have sought soberness then we have risen above it all, and then all wines are ours.

At all times Persia has had great poets and it has been called the land of poetry; in the first place because the Persian language is so well adapted to poetry, but also because all Persian poetry contains a mystical touch. The literary value of the poetry only makes it poetry; but when a mystical value is added this makes the poetry prophecy. The climate. and atmosphere of Persia have also been most helpful to poetry, and the very imaginative nature of the people has made their poetry rich. At all times and in all countries, when the imagination has no scope for expansion, poetry dies and materialism increases.

There is no poet in the world who is not a mystic. A poet is a mystic whether consciously, or unconsciously, for no one can write poetry without inspiration, and when a poet touches the profound depths of the spirit, struck by some aspect of life, he brings forth a poem as a diver brings forth a pearl.

In this age of materialism and ever-growing commercial-ism man seems to have lost the way of inspiration. During my travels I was asked by a well-known writer whether it is really true that there is such a thing as inspiration. This gave me an idea of how far nowadays some writers and poets are removed from inspiration. It is the materialism of the age which is responsible for this; if a person has a tendency towards poetry or music, as soon as he begins to write something his first thought is, 'Will it catch on or not? What will be its practical value?' And generally what catches on is that which appeals to the average man. In this way culture is going downward instead of upward.

When the soul of the poet is intoxicated by the beauty of nature and the harmony of life, it is moved to dance; and the expression of the dance is poetry. The difference between inspired poetry and mechanical writing is as great as the difference between true and false. For long ages the poets of Persia have left a wonderful treasure of thought for humanity. Jelal-ud-Din Rumi has revealed in his *Masnavi* the mystery of profound revelation. In the East his works are considered as sacred as holy scriptures. They have illuminated numberless souls and the study of his work can be considered to belong to the highest standard of culture.

The poet is a creator, and he creates in spite of all that confronts him; he creates a world of his own. And by doing so he rises naturally above that plane where only what is visible and touchable is regarded as real. When he sings to the sun, when he smiles to the moon, when he prays to the sea, and when he looks at the plants, at the forests, and at life in the desert, he communicates with nature. In the eyes of the ordinary person he is imaginative, dreamy, visionary; his thoughts seem to be in the air. But if one asked the poet what he thinks of these others, he would say that it is those who cannot fly who remain on the ground. It is natural that creatures which walk on the earth are not always able to fly; those which fly in the air must have wings, and among human beings one will find that same difference, for in human beings there are all things.

There are souls like germs and worms, there are souls like animals and birds, and there are souls like jinns and angels. Among human beings all can be found: those who belong to the earth, those who dwell in heaven, and those who dwell in the very depths.

Those who were able to soar upward by the power of their imagination have been living poets. What they said was not only a statement, it was music itself; it not only had a rhythm, but it had also a tone in it. It made their souls dance and it would make anyone dance who heard their poetry. Thus Hafiz of Shiraz gives a challenge to the dignified, pious men of his country when he says, 'Pious friends, you would forget your dignity if you would hear the song which came from my glowing heart.' And it is such souls who have touched the highest summits of life, so that they have been able to contribute some truth, giving an interpretation of human nature and the inner law of life.

It is another thing with poets who have made poetry for the sake of fame or name or popularity, or so that it might be appreciated by others; for that is business and not poetry. Poetry is an art, an art of the highest degree. The poet's communication with nature brings him in the end to communicate with himself, and by that communication he delves deeper and deeper, within and without, communicating with life everywhere. This communication brings him into a state of ecstasy, and in his ecstasy his whole being is filled with joy; he forgets the worries and anxieties of life, he rises above the praise and blame of this earth, and the things of this world become of less importance to him. He stands on the earth but gazes into the heavens; his outlook on life becomes broadened and his sight keen. He sees things that no one else is interested in, that no one else sees.

This teaches us that what may be called heaven or paradise is not very far from man. It is always near him, if only he would look at it. Our life is what we look at. If we look at the right thing then it is right; if we look at the wrong thing then it is wrong. Our life made according to our own attitude, and that is why the poet proves to be self-sufficient, and also indifferent and independent; these qualities become wings, for him to fly upward. The poet is in the same position as anyone else in regard to the fears and worries that life brings, the troubles and difficulties that everyone feels in the midst of the world, and yet he rises above these things so that they do not touch him.

No doubt the poet is much more sensitive to the troubles and difficulties of life than an ordinary person. If he took to heart everything that came to him, all the jarring influences that disturbed his peace of mind, all the rough edges of life that everyone has to rub against, he would not be able to go on; but on the other hand if he hardened his heart and made it less sensitive, then he would also close his heart to the inspiration which comes as poetry. Therefore in order to open the doors of his heart, to keep its sensitiveness, the one who communicates with life within and without is open to all influences whether agreeable or disagreeable and is without any protection; and his only escape from all the disturbances of life is through rising above them.

The prophetic message which was given by Zarathushtra (Zoroaster) to the people of Persia was poetic from beginning to end. It is most interesting to see that Zarathushtra showed in his scriptures and all through his life how a poet rises from earth to heaven. It suggests to us how Zarathushtra communicated with nature, with its beauty, and how at every step he took he touched deeper and deeper the depths of life. Zarathushtra formed his religion by praising the beauty in nature and by finding the source of his art which is creation itself in the Artist who is behind it all.

What form of worship did he teach? He taught the same worship with which he began his poetry and with which he finished it. He said to his pupils, 'Stand before the sea, look at the vastness of it, bow before it, before its source and goal.' He said to them, 'Look at the sun, and see what joy it brings. What is at the back of it? Where does it come from? Think of its source and goal, and how you are heading towards it.' People then thought that it was sun-worship, but it was not; it was the worship of light which is the source and goal of all. That communication within and without sometimes extended the range of a poet's vision so much that it was beyond the comprehension of the average man.

When the Shah of Persia said that he would like to have the history of his country written, for one did not exist at that time, Firdausi, a poet who was inspired and intuitive said, 'I will write it and bring it to you.' He began to meditate, throwing his searchlight as far back into the past as possible, and before the appointed time he was able to prepare that book and bring it to the court. It is said that the spiritual power of that poet was so great that when someone at the court sneered at the idea of a man being able to look so far back into the past, he went up to him and put his hand on his forehead and said, 'Now see!' And the man saw with his own eyes that which was written in the book.

This is human; it is not superhuman, although examples of it are rarely to be found; for in the life of every human being, especially of one who is pure-hearted, loving, sympathetic, and good, the past, present, and future are manifested to a certain extent. If one's inner light were thrown back as a searchlight it could go much further than man can comprehend. Some have it to develop this gift, but others are born with it; and among those who are born with it we find some who perhaps know ten or twelve years before and what is going to happen. Therefore a poet is someone who can focus his soul on the past, and also throw his light on the future, and make that clear which has not yet happened but which has been planned beforehand and which already exists in the abstract.

It is such poetry that becomes inspirational poetry. It is through such poetry that the intricate aspects of metaphysics can be taught. All the Upanishads of the Vedas are written in poetry; the suras of the Qu'ran and Zarathushtra's scriptures are all in poetry. All these prophets, whenever they came, brought the message in poetry.

The development of poetry in Persia occurred at a time when there was a great conflict between the orthodox and the free-thinkers. At that time the law of the nation was a religious law and no one was at liberty to express his free thoughts which might be in conflict with the religious ideas. And there were great thinkers such as Firdausi, Farid-ud-Din-Attar, Jelal-ud-Din Rumi, Sa'di, Hafiz, Jami, Omar Khayyam, who were not only poets, but who were poetry itself. They were living in another world although they appeared to be on earth. Their outlook on life, their keen sight, were different to those of everyone else. The words which arose from their hearts were not brought forth with effort, they were natural flames rising up out of the heart. And these words remain as flames enlightening souls of all times, whatever soul they have touched.

Sufism has been the wisdom of these poets. There has never been a poet of note in Persia who was not a Sufi, and every one of them has added a certain aspect to the Sufi ideas, but they took great care not to affront the minds of orthodox people. Therefore a new terminology had to be invented in Persian poetry; the poets had to use words such as 'wine' and 'bowl' and 'beloved' and 'rose', words which would not offend the orthodox mind and would yet at the same time serve as symbolical expressions to explain the divine law." End of quote. (All in brackets, by Paul Smith).

Further Reading...

The Sufi Message of Hazrat Inayat Khan Volume X: Sufi Mysticism; The Path of Initiation and Discipleship; Sufi Poetry, Art: Yesterday, Today and Tomorrow; The Problem of the Day. Barrie and Jenkins, London, 1964. *(Pages 119-154... after the three essays printed above Hazrat Inayat Khan goes on to talk about 'Attar, Rumi, Sadi and Hafiz).*

A History of Ottoman Poetry by E.J.W. Gibb. Volume One, Luzac & Co. Ltd. London 1900. *(Pages 33-69.)*

A Critical Appreciation of Arabic Mystical Poetry by Dr. S.H. Nadeem, Adam Publishers. New Delhi, 2003.

Sufi Poems, A Mediaeval Anthology by Martin Lings, Islamic Texts Society, Cambridge, 2004.

The Way of the Mystics: The Early Christian Mystics and The Rise of the Sufis by Margaret Smith, Sheldon Press, 1976.

In the Garden of Myrtles: Studies in Early Islamic Mysticism by Tor Andrae, Translated by Birgitta Sharpe. State University of New York Press, Albany. 1987.

Muslim Saints and Mystics... Episodes from the 'Memorial of the Saints' by Farid al-Din Attar, Translated by A.J. Arberry. Routledge and Kegan Paul, London, 1966.

Kashf Al-Mahjub of Al-Hujwiri. Translated by R.A. Nicholson, Luzac, London. 1967.

God Speaks: The Theme of Creation and Its Purpose by Meher Baba. Dodd, Mead & Company, New York, 1955. *(Meher Baba in great detail explains the Involution of the Soul and the seven stages of the Spiritual Path, the role of the Perfect Master, the Creation and the different States of God using quotations from Sufi poets and Masters and Sufi terminology and cross-referencing with Christian Mystical and Vedantic terminology.*

The Poetic Forms in Makhfi's *Divan*

The Ruba'i

Many scholars of Persian Poetry believe that the *ruba'i* is the most ancient Persian poetic form that is original to this language and they state that all other classical forms including the *ghazal, kasida, masnavi, kit'a* etc., originated in Arabic literature and the metres employed in them were in Arabic poetry in the beginning... this, can be disputed.

The Persian language is a fine intercourse of Arabic (a masculine-sounding language) and Pahlavi (a feminine-sounding language) which is a descendant of the profound language of the Spiritual Master Zoroaster... Zend. Sanskrit is also a branch of that ancient language* (e.g. Zend: *garema* or heat is in Sanskrit *gharma,* in Pahlavi is *garma,* Persian... *garm,* given to us by that prophet whose perfect and profound teachings in the *gathas* of the *Avesta* were composed in a form very close to the *ruba'i* which one could believe could give him the title not only of the founder of the Persian language and people and mysticism... but also of Persian poetry's most individualistic form of poetic expression.

One can trace the origins of this poetical language back almost 7000 years to Zoroaster's time, not merely less than 3000 years... a mistake that most recent scholars made by confusing the last Zoroastian *priest* bearing his name with that of this original Prophet, the *Rasool* or Messiah, who like Moses, led out his people numbering about 100,000 from their original Aryan lands in Bactria, when they were invaded by many hordes of murderous barbarians.

On that remarkable and in many aspects, far-reaching journey, an argument occurred amongst his people when they had reached what we called (until partition) India, and many left him and settled there and their language eventually evolved into Sanskrit. Zoroaster then took his remaining followers west and finally settled in Fars in south-western Persia, and Zend eventually became Pehlevi and of course the Aryan language continued west and founded many languages in Europe, including English.

Now as to the origin of the rhyme of the *ruba'i*, I offer two of Zoroaster's poems or *gathas* to enjoy and consider, even though the metre may not be that of the *ruba'i*, the rhyme structure and content are similar.

Wise One, with these short poems I come before You,
praising Your Righteousness, deeds of Good Mind too.

And when I arrive at that bliss that has come to me...

may these poems of this man of insight... come through.

And another...

May good rulers and not evil ones over us be ruling!

O devoted, by doing good works for mankind, bring

rebirth... prepare all this for what's good for all men:

through work in the field... let ox for us be fattening.

The *ruba'i* is a poem of four lines in which usually the first, second and fourth lines rhyme and sometimes with the *radif* (refrain) after the rhyme words... sometimes all four rhyme. It is composed in metres called *ruba'i* metres. Each *ruba'i* is a separate poem in itself and should not be regarded as a part of a long poem as was created by FitzGerald when he translated those he attributed to Omar Khayyam, most wrongly.

The *ruba'i* (as its name implies) is two couplets *(beyts)* in length, or four lines *(misra)* as stated. The *ruba'i* is a different metre from those used in Arabic poetry that preceded it.

How was this metre invented? The accepted story of the blind wandering minstrel-dervish Rudaki (d. 941) creating this new *metre* of the *hazaj* group which is essential to the *ruba'i* is as follows... One New Year's Festival he happened to be strolling in a garden where some children played with nuts and one threw a walnut along a groove in a stick and it jumped out then rolled back again creating a sound and the children shouted with delight in imitation, 'Ghaltan ghaltan hami ravad ta bun-i gau,' [Ball, ball, surprising hills... to end of a brave try]. Rudaki immediately recognised in the line's metre a new invention and by the repetition four times of the *rhyme* he had quickly created the *ruba'i*... and is considered the first master of this form and the father of classical Persian Poetry.

Shams-e Qais writing two hundred years later about this moment of poetic history and the effect of this new form on the population said the following... "This new poetic form fascinated all classes, rich and poor, ascetic and drunken rebel-outsider[rend], all wanted to participate in it... the sinful and the good both loved it; those who were so ignorant they couldn't make out the difference between poetry and prose began to dance to it; those with dead hearts who couldn't tell the difference between a donkey braying and reed's wailing and were a thousand miles away from listening to a lute's strumming, offered up their souls for a *ruba'i*. Many young cloistered girls, from passion for the song of a *ruba'i* broke down the doors, *and* their chastity's walls; many matrons from love for a *ruba'i* let loose the braids of their self-restraint."

And so, the *ruba'i* should be eloquent, spontaneous and ingenious. In the *ruba'i* the first three lines serve as an introduction to the fourth that should be sublime, subtle or pithy and clever. As can be seen from the quote by Shams-e Qais above, the *ruba'i* immediately appealed to all levels of society and has done so ever since. The nobility and royalty enjoyed those in praise of them and the commoner enjoyed the short, simple homilies… the ascetic and mystic could think upon epigrams of deep religious fervour and wisdom; the reprobates enjoyed the subtle and amusing satires and obscenities… and for everyone, especially the cloistered girls and old maids, many erotic and beautiful love poems to satisfy any passionate heart.

Almost every major and minor poet in Persia composed at some time in the *ruba'i* form.

Note: See 'Comparative Grammar, Lecture 6' in 'Lectures on the Science of Language' 1861 By Max Muller, Reprint Munshi Ram Manohar Lal, Delhi, 1965.

The Ghazal.

There is really no equivalent to the *ghazal* (pronounced *guz'el*) in English poetry… although as Masud Farzaad, the greatest Iranian authority on Hafiz and his *ghazals* said, the sonnet is probably the closest. As a matter of fact, the *ghazal* is a unique form and its origin has been argued about for many centuries.

Some say that the *ghazal* originated in songs that were composed in Persia to be sung at court before Persia was converted to Islam, but not one song has survived to prove this. It is also possible that originally the *ghazals* were songs of love that were sung by minstrels in the early days of Persian history and that this form passed into poetry down the ages. I find this explanation plausible for the following reasons: firstly, the word *ghazal* means 'a conversation between lovers'. Secondly, the *ghazals* of Hafiz, Sadi and others were often put to music and became songs, which have been popular in Persia from ancient times until now.

Other scholars see the *ghazal* as coming from Arabic poetry, especially the prelude to longer poems, i.e. the *kasida:* they say that this prelude was isolated and changed, to eventually become the *ghazal*. The Arabic root of the word *ghazal* is *gazl* which means: spinning, spun, thread, twist... the form of the *ghazal* is a spiral. Hazrat Ali's *ghazal* in this volume seems to confirm that it was originally of Arabic creation.

Whatever the origin, by the fourteenth century the *ghazal* had become a mature form of poetry. Among the great *ghazal* writers in Persian of the past were Nizami, Farid ad-Din 'Attar, Rumi, and Sadi and in Turkish, Yunus Emre; but with the *ghazals* of Hafiz and other poets in Shiraz during his lifetime this form reached its summit.

The form of the *ghazal* at first glance seems simple, but on a deeper inspection it will be found that there is more to it than one at first sees.

It is usually between five and fifteen couplets (*beyts* or 'houses'), but sometimes more. A *beyt* is 'a line of verse split into two equal parts scanning exactly alike.' Each couplet has a fixed rhyme which appears at the end of the second line. In the first couplet which is called the *matla* meaning 'orient' or 'rising,' the rhyme appears at the end of both lines. This first couplet has the function of 'setting the stage' or stating the subject matter and feeling of the poem. The other couplets or *beyts* have other names depending on their positions. One could say that the opening couplet is the subject, the following couplets the actions: changing, viewed from different angles, progressing from one point to another, larger and deeper, until the objective of the poem is reached in the last couplet. The final couplet is known as the *maqta* or 'point of section.' This couplet or the one before it, almost always contains the *takhallus* or pen-name of the poet, signifying that it was written by him and also allowing him the chance to detach himself from himself and comment on what effect the actions of the subject matter in the preceding couplets had on him. Often the poet uses a play on words when he uses his own pen-name... ('Hafiz' for example, means: a preserver, a guardian, rememberer, watchman, one who knows the *Koran* by heart. 'Makhfi' means: veiled).

In the *ghazal* the Arabic, Persian, Turkish and Urdu Master Sufi Poets found the ideal instrument to express the great tension between the opposites that exist in this world. Having the strict rhyming structure of the same rhyme at the end of the second line of each couplet (after the first couplet) the mind must continually come back to the world and the poem and the rhyme. But by being allowed to use any word at the end of the first line of each couplet, one can be as spontaneous as possible and give the heart its full rein. This of course happens also in the first line of the first couplet, for whatever word or rhyme-sound that comes out in the first line sets the rhyme for the rest of the *ghazal*. So the 'feeling' created by the rhyme is one that comes spontaneously from the heart, and this spontaneity is allowed to be expanded from then on in the non-rhyming lines, and to contract in those lines that rhyme, when the mind must function as an 'orderer' of the poem. This expansion and contraction, feeling and thinking, heart and mind, combine to produce great tension and power that spirals inward and outward and creates an atmosphere that I would define as 'deep nostalgia.' This deep nostalgia is a primal moving force that flows through all life, art and song, and produces within whoever comes into contact with it when it is consciously expressed, an irresistible yearning to unite the opposites that it contains. In the *ghazal* any metre can be employed except the *ruba'i* metre.

The true meaning of Sufism, apart from the recognition of God in human form as the *Qutub* or the *Rasool* or the Christ is *tassawuf*... which means to get to the essence of everything. Adam was the first poet and it is said that he named everything and invented the first alphabet from which all others come. But Adam was not only the creator of conscious language as we know it, he was also the creator of song and the perfect form through which he created songs in praise of Eve his true Beloved, her beauty was displayed in the spiral form of the *ghazal*. So, the *ghazals* he composed and sung to her before their eventual Spiritual Union were of longing and separation and those after... of the bliss of Union. He used the same form of song about other events including the great sorrow and deep nostalgia about the loss of his favourite son Abel.

Two of Arabia's most careful and serious historians Tabari (d.923) and Masudi (d.957) state that the first poem ever composed in known history was one by Adam (the original Sufi

Qutub or First Perfect Master... God-man) on the death of Abel and the form was the *ghazal*...

> *The lands are changed and all those who live upon them,*
> *the face of the earth is torn and surrounded with gloom;*
> *everything that was lovely and fragrant has now faded,*
> *from that beautiful face has vanished the joyful bloom.*
> *What deep regrets for my dear son... O regrets for Abel,*
> *a victim of murder... who has been placed into the tomb!*
> *Is it possible to rest, while that Devil that was cursed*
> *who never fails or dies... up from behind us does loom?*
> *"Give up these lands and all of those who live on them;*
> *I was the one who forced you out of Paradise, your room,*
> *where you and your wife were so secure and established,*
> *where your heart did not know of the world's dark doom!*
> *But you, you did escape all of my traps and my trickery,*
> *until that great gift of life... upon which you did presume*
> *you went and lost... and from Aden the blasts of wind,*
> *but for God's Grace would have swept you like a broom.*

It is said that thousands of years after Adam, the Perfect Spiritual Master Noah, settled Shiraz after his ark landed in the Turkish lands on the mountains of Ararat and was a vintner who brought the first vines that he carried with him was also a poet who composed in this form as did the *Qutub* of some three thousand years later who also settled his people he had led from their homeland in Bactria (northern Afghanistan) to Fars (Persia)... Zoroaster.

His *gathas* or hymns are in rhyme-structure the first two couplets of the *ghazal* which would later be known as the *ruba'i*. And so the *ghazals* of the Zoroastrians were sung in their winehouses and fire temples throughout our land until the Muslim Arabs invaded and converted most to Islam, but poets and minstrels would not give up their much loved eternal God-given *ghazal* or the wine of Noah as well, which had its distant progeny in the *mesqali* grape.

The clandestine winehouses run by the Zoroastrians and Christians became the venues for many hundreds of years of the *ghazal*. In these winehouses Persians could criticise their Arab and Turkish rulers and their police chiefs and false Sufi masters and hypocritical clergy who censored and forbade them to practice the drinking of wine and the appreciation of beautiful faces and forms of unveiled women and handsome young men.

In the winehouses the truth could be told and this truth was quickly spread by the minstrels in the market places and even at court through what was becoming a popular form of expression amongst the masses. And although in fact the actual drinking of wine finally became less because of the religious restrictions, it as a symbol of truth, love and freedom became more widespread.

Of course there always existed another 'Winehouse' where the Wine of Divine Love and Grace was poured out by the Winebringer or *Qutub*, the Perfect Master or the Old Magian. Here the wine and truth that flowed freely from heart to heart was of the spiritual nature and made the lover or drunkard so intoxicated with the Divine Beloved that he became *mast-like*... mad with longing to be united with the Eternal One, Whose beauty he saw and appreciated in the face and form and personality of his earthly beloved whom he praised, wooed, begged, cajoled, described, desired and desperately longed for through his *ghazals* and by his actions and with each breath of his whole life he came closer to the Eternal Beloved. Although the poets of the *ghazal* may appear to many as open-minded, drunken, outcast lovers, it does not necessarily mean that they all drank the juice of the grape... for it is an inner state that they often were expressing. The *ghazal* is a conversation between the lover and the beloved and as in all intimate conversation... the talk flows both ways. The subject may not necessary be about love, but it is always from the point of view of one who loves truth, love and beauty.

SELECTED BIBLIOGRAPHY

Dewan of Zeb-un-Nissa by Magan Lal & Jessie Duncan Westbrook, John Murray Publishers 1913, reprint Orientalia Lahore, 1954.

Makhfi: The Princess Sufi Poet Zeb-un-Nissa: A Selection of Poems from her Divan, Translation & Introduction Paul Smith, New Humanity Books 2012.

The Tears of Zebunnissa: Being excerpts from the Divan-i Makhfi. Metrically Rendered into Eglish by Paul Whalley, M.A.W. Thacker & Co. London 1913.

Captive Princess: Zebunissa, Daughter of Emperor Aurangzeb by Annie Krieger-Krynicki Oxford University Press Karachi, 2003. (Her life story in much detail; but, surprisingly not much about her poetry).

Princesses, Sufis, Dervishes, Martyrs & Feminists: Nine Great Women Poets of the East, Translations, Introductions, Notes by Paul Smith, New Humanity Books, Campbells Creek, 2012.

The Divine Wine: A Treasury of Sufi and Dervish Poetry, Volume Two: Translations, Introductions & Notes by Paul Smith, New Humanity Books, Campbells Creek 2009 (Sections on Makhfi, Nasir Ali & Dara Shikoh).

Piercing Pearls: The Complete Anthology of Persian Poetry: Volume Two: Court, Sufi, Dervish, Satirical, Ribald, Prison & Social Poetry from the 13th Century to Modern Times. Translations & Introduction by Paul Smith, New Humanity Books, Campbell's Creek. 2010. (Sections on Makhfi, Nasir Ali And Dara Shikoh).

History of Iranian Literature. Jan Rypka et al. D. Reidel Publishing Company, Dordrecht. 1968. (Page 729).

Four Eminent Poetesses of Iran, with a brief survey of Iranian and Indian Poetesses of Neo-Persian by M. Ishaque, Calcutta 1950.

A Golden Treasury of Persian Poetry by Hadi Hasan. Indian Council for Cultural Relations, New Delhi, 1966. (P.p. 402-6).

Ruba'iyat of Sarmad, Translation, Introduction by Paul Smith, New Humanity Books, Campbells Creek, 2010.

Ruba'iyat of Dara Shikoh, Translation & Introduction by Paul Smith, New Humanity Books, Campbells Creek, 2012.

Three Sufi-Martyr Poets of India: Sarmad, Dara Shikoh & Makhfi, Translation & Introduction by Paul Smith, New Humanity Books 2014.

GLOSSARY

NOTE: Please read this Glossary carefully before reading the following poems so that the spiritual meaning of this poetry may be understood. As there are many shades and levels of meaning in Sufi Poetry it is necessary to understand the symbols in the context of each poem. Sometimes the poet uses the symbols in a spiritual sense, sometimes in a physical sense and sometimes both. I have not arranged this Glossary alphabetically as is usual, but in a manner which I hope the reader will find less boring and more enjoyable and enlightening.

THE SKY: Sometimes the sky is described as an 'inverted bowl' and 'the blue dome.' The sky symbolises fate: unpredictable, untrustworthy, always changing.

THE SUN: The Beloved, God. The bright face of the Beloved. The Power of God's Light revealing the Truth.

THE MOON: The Beauty of the true Beloved also (in context) the false beauty of the Creation, physical beauty. The Moon cannot be seen unless the light of the Sun is upon it (i.e. the Light of God). The sickle-shaped Moon represents the bent shape of the poor suffering lover and when waning, old age and death. The half (split) Moon symbolises the opposites existing in the psyche, and throughout Creation. The full Moon usually means the Beloved, showing fully the Beauty of God.

VENUS: Music, dance and song. The sky's minstrel. Good fortune.

PLEIADES: Sometimes used as a symbol for the tears of the lover and sometimes as a necklace of jewels to place around the Beloved's neck. Other meanings in context.

THE WIND: The bringer of bad news, misfortune. Sometimes it symbolises one who brings news of death.

THE BREEZE: The bringer of messages from and to the Beloved. Often the messenger who brings good news. Divine inspiration.

THE SEA: The ocean of love to be crossed by the lover. The immensity of Divine Love, of which human love is but a mere drop. The turbulent sea represents the difficulties the lover must endure on the voyage to God.

THE BOAT: The form, energy and mind of the lover of God of whom the Perfect Master is the Captain. Sometimes the boat represents the Perfect Master who sails us to the Divine Shore.

THE PEARL DIVER: The lover of God, the seeker of the Truth.

THE PEARL: God, Divine Knowledge, the Truth, the lover's true Self.

THE SHELL: The outer form, the physical illusion, the false, the ego.

THE DESERT: The long period that the lover of God must pass through when the lover's thirst for God's Grace remains unquenched.

THE HILLS AND VALLEYS: The ups and downs experienced by the lover on the Path of Love.

THE FIELD: The world, whereupon the Game of Love is played.

POLO: The poets sometimes use the game of Polo as a symbol for the Game of Love. The horseman represents the Beloved and the ball symbolizes the lover's mind and sometimes the lover's heart. The Beloved's long curling hair symbolizes the polo-mallet that strikes the ball (the lover's heart).

THE GARDEN: The special place in the world (and in the inner realms) where the lovers see, meet and converse with the Beloved. The Presence of the Beloved.

THE ROSE: The true Beloved, i.e. God. The Perfect Master whose heart has expanded like the rose. Sometimes the rose signifies a beautiful woman. The rosebud sometimes signifies the lover, whose heart has yet to become expanded by Divine Love, i.e. love that is still young.

ROSEWATER: The Grace of God. Divine Mercy. Kindness shown by the Perfect Master.

THE TULIP: The humble, faithful, tragic lover of God. The tulip, blood-streaked, cup-shaped, often symbolizes the heart of the grief-stricken lover.

THE VIOLET: The patient obedient servant or disciple of the Perfect Master (the rose). In Persian gardens violets are often planted in rows leading up to the rosebushes, i.e. like attendants, or lovers waiting to serve the Beloved.

THE HYACINTH: The Beloved's hair is often compared to the hyacinth because of its beautiful perfume.

THE LILY: The lily often symbolises a gossip, its long yellow stamen representing a tongue.

THE ARGHAVAN: The arghavan or Judas tree has crimson flowers. This represents the mature, long-suffering lover.

THE NARCISSUS: A proud beautiful one, jealous of the Beloved's (the rose's) beauty. Sometimes Hafiz refers to the Beloved as the narcissus, telling the Beloved not to be so proud and to call on the lover. Often the eyes of the Beloved are symbolised by the narcissus.

THE CYPRESS: The cypress symbolises the form of the Beloved because of the tall, upright stature of the cypress and because like God Who never changes, the cypress remains green all throughout the year.

THE NIGHTINGALE: The lover of the Beloved (the rose). It also symbolises the poet who sings of the beauty of the Beloved.

THE PARROT: The poet who talks to the Beloved in the hope that the Beloved will reward him with sugar (Love, Grace).

THE FALCON: God. The Perfect Master or the Beloved, who preys upon the lover who is a mere fly by comparison.

THE KITE AND THE CROW: Ignorance, false poets, false masters.

THE PARTRIDGE: False pride, pomposity. Often the partridge symbolises an earthly king, or person in power, who prides himself on his position.

THE HOOPOE OR LAPWING: The messenger of the Perfect Master. A faithful servant.

THE MOTH: The lover, who wishes to extinguish himself in the flame (Love) of the candle (God).

THE PATH, STREET, HIGHWAY: The Path of the love of God in human form i.e. the Perfect Master. The Spiritual way. The path that leads to the Winehouse, wherein is found the Perfect Master. The journey through the inner realms of consciousness to the true Self (God).

THE WINEHOUSE: The place where the lover goes to be with the Beloved, the Perfect Master. The dwelling of the Perfect Master. Sometimes the Winehouse symbolises the inner Self of the lover.

THE WINE: Truth, Love, Grace, Knowledge. As ordinary wine changes a person's personality, so Divine Wine changes the inner consciousness and brings the lover closer to God and intoxicates the lover with God's Love and Truth. The more the lover drinks of this wine, the more he becomes addicted to it and the more he loses his reasoning. Wine (in the ordinary sense) was forbidden to Muslims and by using wine as a symbol for personal love for God and from God (as Jesus did), the poets point out the difference between formal and personal religion. The love for the Perfect Master that the poet advocated could result in persecution by the orthodox clergy of the time: hence, the symbol was an apt one.

THE CUP: The heart of the lover of God and sometimes the Beloved, from whom flows the wine of Divine Love.

THE FLAGON AND WINECASK: The Perfect Master.

THE WINEBRINGER: The Beloved, the Perfect Master, the Godman, or anyone who brings to the lover (the drunkard) God's Love, Truth and Beauty... sometimes Destiny, which brings the cup from which we must drink.

THE FRIEND: God, the Perfect Master.

THE BELOVED: God, the Perfect Master. God perceived in beautiful human form.

THE BELOVED'S HAIR: The attraction of God's Grace. The Mystery that conceals the Divine Essence. The hair sometimes symbolises the world with its problems (tangles) and mysteries, in which sometimes we get trapped.

THE BELOVED'S CURLS: The beauties of God's Manifestation. The charms of Beloved. The twists of Fate.

THE BELOVED'S EYE: The Power of God. One glance and we can become annihilated in His Love.

THE BELOVED'S EYEBROW: The eyebrow of the Beloved is often compared with the arch towards which one prays (in the direction of Mecca) in a Mosque.

THE BELOVED'S DOWN (ON CHEEK OR LIP): This symbolizes the attractions of Divine Love. It also symbolises the sprouting forth of Life.

THE BELOVED'S LIP: The lip of the Beloved will heal the lover because from it the lover can taste the Water of Everlasting Life and the Wine of Divine Love.

THE BELOVED'S MOLE: An attraction of the Beloved, full of Mystery. The Perfect imperfection?

THE WINEMAKER: God in human form; the Messiah, Rasool, Avatar e.g. Adam, Jesus, Mohammed, Noah.

THE WINESELLER: The Perfect Master.

THE KING, SOVEREIGN, MONARCH: God in human form, same as above. The pots often use these titles when speaking of the Perfect Master. By using such symbology they could openly praise the Master and the king of the time would not be jealous, but pleased, for he would think that they were about him.

MONARCH'S CROWN: God's Glory.

THE SLAVE: The lover of God (the King), who is bound by God's Beauty, which is sometimes represented by the long flowing (chainlike) hair of the Beloved.

THE PAINTER, THE ARCHITECT: God the Creator.

THE RUIN: This world, wherein one can find the Treasure (the Perfect Master, the Truth). It also symbolises the lover's body which though ruined through searching and longing for God, still contains the jewel of the Soul.

THE INN, HOTEL: The world, where we must stay awhile before passing on.

THE SUFI: The Muslim mystic. Some poets talk of true and false Sufis as many of the 'Sufi Orders' had become corrupted by the 13th century... and remain so today, sometimes full of rituals and false 'masters'.

THE SUFI'S GARMENT: The poets advise us to soak our coat of religion in the wine of Divine Love.

THE DERVISH: The true lover of God, the real mystic.

THE KALANDAR: Like the dervish, a true lover of God, but also a wanderer.

THE REND (RIND): The drunken outsider, the reprobate in the population's eyes but really the true lover of God.

KHIZER: A particular kind of Perfect Spiritual Master *(Qutub)* or the Prophet or Messiah or Avatar *(Rasool)* who has gained immortality and the ability to appear anywhere at any time in another form or to direct someone who hasn't a Master to do his bidding or someone who is consciously or unconsciously used by the Master (who becomes 'Khizer') to direct one without a Master to the Master, or... the 'Water of Life'.

A Note on This Translation

In the Persian language there is no 'she' or 'he'... only *'oo'* or the person or object referred to... i.e. 'you' or 'that one'. Most translators wrongly either use 'he' or she' depending on their interpretations. I have not done this. Usually Makhfi is addressing the Divine Beloved (or Spiritual Master or *'Qutub'* in Sufi terminology) and occasionally an earthly beloved, so I make the judgment as to which and either capitalize or not, as in 'You' and 'you', 'that one' and 'that One'.

Ruba'is...

Love… the marauder, ties to his saddle's bows
all the scalps of his countless, slaughtered foes.
Look, at how with blood of mankind Love
painted on the earth's forehead, a crimson rose.

O waterfall... for sake of who, weeping are you?
You have wrinkled your brows, grieving for who?
What agony caused you all night long, like me to
hit your head upon stone and weep like me, too?

I the hunted, have no peace, a Hunter chases me;
it is my remembrance of You... when I turn to flee
I fall, You throw a snare... Your perfumed hair:
none escape, from dreams of You no heart is free!

I am tired of life… and life is tired of me:
like glass and stone… describes our company.
How can I come to Beloved's tent?
Road's dark, and my horse is tiring badly!

Nightingale would turn from rose if seeing me,
and Brahmin would no longer idol pray to daily!
Like the fragrance in roses I hide... in my poetry,
who would know me must in it me, try to see!

I don't want beauty; it is inner truth I'm

seeking:

love's slave, all faiths and mysteries I'm

sharing!

Preacher, don't tell me about Hell's pain,

worst pain of Hell inside this heart... I'm

bearing!

I'm no moth, that in some impetuous way
flies into a flame and dies... better to say
I am a candle that with an inner passion
slowly and silently, keeps burning away.

You who seized in Your curls like chains, lover's heart,

whose marvellous beauty bewilders mind... for a start,

in pit of Your dimpled chin those loyal will find fountain Khizer* searched for ages for... a mere upstart!

*Note: Khizer...A particular kind of Perfect Spiritual Master (Qutub) or the Prophet or Messiah or Avatar (Rasool) who has gained immortality and the ability to appear anywhere at any time in another form or to direct someone who hasn't a Master to do his bidding or someone who is consciously or unconsciously used by the Master (who becomes 'Khizer') to direct one without a Master to the Master, or... the 'Water of Life'. See my 'Khider in Sufi Poetry', New Humanity Books, 2012.

Ghazals...

First, to You, Whose merciful clouds births my garden's rose, I see:

lets praise of Your Love, beautify the first couplet of my *Divan*, purposely.

My body and soul thirst for Your Love and like Mansur* every grain of this dusty body cries, "We are a part, You're all, we're Divinity!"

Waves of Your Love's deluge roll over the boat of destruction: my soul drowned in love's depth a Noah could not lift to float free.

For me the powers of darkness like slaves will obediently fly off if one word of my praises You accept... then like Solomon I will be!

And now, not so easily do tears begin like cries off my tongue, for drops of blood from my heart as pearls on my lashes all can see.

Makhfi, bear with patience your pain that is endless and your night of passion... only then Khizer spring of joy with you will be.

Note: Mansur Hallaj (d.919 A.D.), who was sentenced to death for saying: "I am the Truth (Anal Haq)." On Mansur Hallaj's life and sayings see: 'Muslim Saints and Mystics' by Farid ud-Din Attar trans. by A.J. Arberry R.K.P. pp. 264-272; and for his poems my 'Mansur Hallaj: Selected Poems' New Humanity Books, 2012.

You, Who all human and divine made, by Your grace we're living:
may this torch of hope You gave us, continue… to keep on shining.
Your love ferments inside us as Your streams of mercy run:
look down and bless Mohammed… and everything he was doing.
Whether it be in *Kaaba* at Mecca or temple pilgrims visit…
You will remain my God, no matter where God someone is worshipping.
I'll welcome the morning with sighs and tears and from my heart burning a sacred fire a breath rises, my desire's mirror burnishing!
Makhfi, drop your tears here… their quenching torrents rain on my heart burning with pain so hot… flames flare as I am sighing!

O Prophet, over the world your soul over-powering banner's unfurled...
witness how your religion spread until Persia and Arabia are led.

Your lips open like rosebuds and flowing are your wise words not only to humans, but birds sing out in garden their golden thread.

O you whose beauty I with great happiness witness, it's true that Nature's never created such youthfulness: beauty to be loved.

Such loveliness trapped me so well that I'd gladly, patiently tread renunciation's path... be off to go wherever your feet led.

But how can I my poor heart's joy deny or give up the grief that I cherish... for my sore heart love's cruelty has slowly bled.

See where from wounds flows a crimson flood, but fragrant roses grow, thorns tearing my wandering feet into roses are turned.

O Makhfi, if the keeper of the *Kaaba* shuts the door on you do not complain... you have a holier place, never fear being spurned...

look deep in eyes of Beloved's face: above eyes arise arches
fairer than *Kaaba's* gates: bend heart, an archway to Friend,
instead.

Love's path is here... winding, long, dark with many a snare;
yet eager pilgrims throng, like doves the fowler's net to share.
What grain lured the dove? The mole on the fair cheek!
What wove love's net? The loose curls of the Beloved's hair!
Love's festival's held here, cup passes, drink this wine:
yes, drain it to the dregs... never of drunkenness divine beware!
Easy to sigh, complain: the world weeps to relieve woe!
Hold pain proudly in heart, silently take poison of grief, despair.
You are light's source, paradise's fount, eternal grace;
brighter than Moses off the mount, God's radiance to share.
Night's wine 'til dawn offers exultation, morn to night
offers back its dream so happy soul's delight never ends anywhere.
Makhfi, where's the feast... merry-makers? See, apart!
In my soul God's feast's laid, here in my heart's secret chamber.

Heart's treasure is stolen, I'm ashamed I left it unguarded, carelessly...
now I am weeping feeling I've been robbed, but blame is on me!
I lit altar's fire with my hands: heart's fire like lamp's flame glows even through body encasing it, as with desire it burns fiercely.
If I turn foolish heart to ashes then rest my grief might end:
I turn towards the ocean of Your love to find inside it peace, gratefully.
In its waters I sink... to its surface my tired limbs can't go:
in depth of ocean of Your love I drown, waves lap, drifting me.
My lonely heart was in the wild until love transformed it,
and now it shines as brightly as the gardens of Paradise... divinely.
I'd like to pour out my longing, turn my grief into psalms...
my pain could be sung, like sweet-singing David of Israel, sublimely.
I go into the field like a bird to peck up ears of golden grain,
but not corn... only tears I gather, see... like rain they fall profusely.

Sage: "Be happy at love's feast, carefully guard winecup."
"O sage, from ecstasy I drank my share, your own guard closely!"
Makhfi, your eyes are heavy with sleep: though your tale's not finished such slumber on your soul lies, look for its rest immediately.

When the spring rains come the rivers of sap through trees are
rising
like Your love in my veins, to my heart's most tender tendrils
flowing.
At my hard heart I hit 'til a divine spark of eternal fire flies,
and from it I see rising, Your love's lightning... my heart's
longing!
O weak of faith come, help is here! See our heart's flashes!
If you had faith's eye, they'd seem like Sinai's white light
shining!
Come... love's feast is spread, share cup we deeply drink:
see the wine... tears shed, wine-cups are our eyes, forever
weeping.
While drinking, on us falls... spell, dream, vision, ecstasy:
pain's wine turns blood... we can't tell if we are or aren't,
existing.
In jungle of this world of woe desire's lion stalks, hungry.
Our faith girding us, like hunter we go... if we resist he is
fleeing!
Often my heart sings praises, through rapturous days...
ah no, voice evil powers chokes, blasting thought, songs
destroying!

Beloved, from glance You gave beauty flows, words can't express:
this life, it was so little to offer... out of thanks for Your bountifulness.
Pious assembly was ashamed, hearts grieved when they heard from love for Your wild curls far away nations felt restlessness.
My heart's broken into pieces, ravaged by tears of grief, but to lover Your lashes wounded relief never comes to caress.
Proud Beloved, at Your feet I lay brow's pride; I am as near Your heart as Your coat, why "You're a stranger," express?
O Makhfi, like Majnun* walk proudly in grief's valley with new dedication gird yourself, love's promise... no less!

Note: Majnun (about 721 A.D.) which means 'madman' whose real name was Qays, was the famous lover of Layla who came from another tribe in Arabia. Majnun fell in love with Layla when they were children at school together. Unable to contain his love, one day he expressed it and Layla's father, enraged by the scandal of this 'madman' in love with his daughter, refused to allow them to see etch other. Majnun's father, who was the leader of his tribe, tried to reconcile them but to no avail. Layla also loved Majnun. Majnun wandered the hills living with wild animals and composing songs in praise of Layla. Finally their human love became so great that it was transformed into Divine Love by a Perfect Master. Layla became so undernourished that she finally starved to death. Majnun threw himself on his grave and died there. Their souls mingled with their dust. Many stories and poems have been written about them, the most popular being those by Nizami and Fuzuli. Possibly their story which came through Spain into Europe inspired Massuccio Salernitano whose story inspired Luigi Da Porto, whose story inspired Shakespeare to write his play Romeo and Juliet. See my translation of 'Layla & Majnun by Nizami' New Humanity Books. 2010 and my 'Poems of Majnun', New Humanity Books, 2012.

O Winebringer, do it: in this moon-like goblet pour wine like sun
from dusky flask 'til overflowing like dawn's clouds: night's done.
See my unlucky heart, broken, dissolving with pain as tears
in my lashes; yet I can't leave it, slithers stay: I wait 'til it is none.
Long ago I knew your promises were a fake, ignoring them.
Why was I born into an age so of love ungrateful, fate… in oblivion?
Ah, but Makhfi, grasp your joy, who knows what awaits?
Earth may shake, wind might blow empty life, vain bubble jettison.

I want not fortune or power from Heaven, only briefly a garden apart

where we can live near what is divine... in love of friends of my heart.

In rapture nightingale sings to rose in centre of the new garden: only Gardener creates beauty; in heat working, into feet thorns dart.

Beauty is immortal, like the sun's might lighting all the worlds and creations made with joy of its light... we thank You for all Art!

And thanks for the great Masters that are given to guide and lead us in our need, their presence safe shelter and shade does impart.

Mercy! See us, weak, sick, sad: so when we seek oblivion and You know time's defeated us, save us from again being of it a part.

The Master who knows that good and evil are one is happy... that one's centred, shaken by none: the rose of spring and the counterpart

autumn plays are one to that one... he is beyond being taught, or, ignorant one, being preached to... to him you've no help to impart!

If you are led by dangerous love and enter the Masters path,

in desert like Majnun you'll stay always, never to look back: start

to know this, you'll not even care if you lose your life or not,

pain ignore, not to seek shore of love's limitless ocean you'll depart.

O Makhfi, like baby birds fall from nest, fluttering, helpless,

caught in nets… see like others are you, too boldly you flew apart

you thought you were… and yet those feeble wings of yours

failed, now you wail your fate, caught in net of your cares… upstart!

*Waken, get up my soul, for it is spring:
let narcissus with its divine scent bring
its sorcery and then let the winebringer
bring idol, wine that one's worshipping.
Do not turn from this forbidden path...
and... O tyrannical Beloved, be looking
on Your victims trampled in Your pride
who for a look would be happily dying!
Some pay their worship at the Kaaba,
others in Temples apart are praying...
Makhfi, think what secret joy is yours,
always in your heart, your Idol having!*

Why argue about whether on Mount Sinai divine radiance is
shining?
Reason's beyond me: though world denies it, my heart it... is
knowing!
My heart is hot: yes... it's burst into flames of love so fierce
that all the Nile's flooding would be like a drop, to stop my
thirsting!
I'm so deep in sin I can't make my way where holy pilgrims
go to Mecca, even if God's friend, Abraham... me be there
leading!
I've wisdom's kingdom... it tires me, I'm bored with reason:
O passion of love, carry me to that one, a hundred miles be
travelling.
See, I come to the water's side, the obedient waves go back:
this flaming heart of mine fire will guide like Moses' torch...
exulting!
Though I've evil days with no joy, with never-ending pain,
do your worst O Fate, for still... Friend beyond friends, is
remaining.
O Makhfi, tell me... is it I who sins? Is this my sin I bear?
It is the body or soul inside that lived, and elsewhere was
sinning?

O my foolish heart, how can I begin to understand your carelessness?
You've no power to remove what from Friend separates us?
See how rosebud coming out from her torn green dress is so beautiful in garden, as was Joseph in his youthful loveliness!
Go spring breeze… quickly tell Jacob, blinded by tears, news to end grief and dark of his worrying years… no less!
Fortunate, more blessed than Alexander's lot, is mine: come, thirsty ones: my fate… to know giver of wine of holiness!
I've wiped heart clean from actions, yes, and desires… alone, I seek peace: at Final Day, not hell or heaven, I stress!

See my heart's fire glow... my sighs fanned it, until it, flames rekindled...

body, weak cage, can't stop bird's flutter: soul longs to not be imprisoned.

Rocks would melt, becoming flowing tears if my never-ending tale of woe they heard, in heart's dark a bell clangs... caravan's assembled.

Love, for years I cried of your tyranny, none heard, just saw my tears; now, poor but proud, Hatim's* table of eager crowd I've abandoned!

Look, I sat through separation's night as heart's delight never appeared as bloody tears from my widowed heart gushed. then flooded!

And yet... still in me, so purged by grief, hope rises and my withered wreath, into scented flowers of Paradise, are then changed!

I'm cruelly bound by these chains by Love, my faith in You: at Your feet like a beaten dog I beg for crumbs of Your love, trained!

O Makhfi, if your sighs could reach sea's breast, even in the cold, still, deep, from your heart a fire unquenched, will have leaped!

*Note: Hatim Tai, an Arabian chief from famous for generosity.

Love, I'm your slave: like as on tulip's burning petal a spot glows...
so in my heart a more passionate flower with darker stain grows.
I'm proud I sought world's rose, still fresh, eager in quest,
not fainting nor failing nor complaining, head held high, it shows!
Blessed pain, grief, sweet no sleep, undying desire, I keep!
Heart torn to bits... for soul's bright diamond my longing flows.
See light from Your merciful torch blessing heart's garden,
Blessed One, its radiance on my wall's shadow, even sun outglows.
I humbly sit apart... as true believers tread to courts of the
Kaaba: not mixing my praise with theirs, I'm outside from those
and all their prayers for all the fibres of my sacred thread
are more precious to God... as He sees love that in heart grows.
O Makhfi, so sorrowful, from the valley of despair and of
pain look out... for the breath of love the morning breeze blows...

and pearls from your eyelids fall like gentle rain upon the garden summoning up the rose, calling up the spring that glows.

Lost its taste has the wine of my delight...
my existence's earth is just a wasted site,
no healthy grass grows there, only weeds;
that my fair spring of life is gone, is right.
I sought out joy but never found an end...
my empty hands no friend can hold tight!
And if to me God's pardon never comes,
my prayers are but dead grass... a blight!
But, Makhfi, look with a discerning eye:
bliss, might than despair need... insight!
Though on love's path your feet may tire,
new power comes, a new desire, delight!

O desolate one, when will you again the garden
see?
Keep inside you, your heart's garden, apart and
holy:
like bird caged for ages forgets flying, songs of
the wild... wings outstretched, makes cage its
totality.
Your love is one with you, so you have no fear
(heart held in love's net) of separation's bitter
agony.
We wait and tire, sight of Beloved vainly desire
until in our heart hope of Resurrection comes...
suddenly.
O heart, yours is not less than Brahmin's faith,
knotted veins his thin form bears or his thread,
holy.
A lover's fate is...? What comes to the unlucky?
The world will cry upon a whim: "Crucify him,"
ignorantly.
Why then complain, on you drags a heavy chain?
No, it fits you to wear such weight, learn to bear
patiently.

As, far from here, Farhad despaired, weary of life,
welcoming kind death and wept, so for relief weep
profusely.
See thorny desert where your cut feet traced path
of lovers, soaked in blood, blooming like a rose...
fragrantly.
Love, I'll complain of death's noose you request?
No, if Your glory gains, I am all pain suffering...
proudly.
O Makhfi, if your fate is without any garden...
in desolation to be dwelling, then it's nothing, a
fantasy...
life's a dream and we that seem to live and move
and love are no more than on a wall, shadows to
see.

The kings, their regal seat were safely keeping,
the poison of defeat they were not yet tasting,
until the Turks their invading army brought…
and from each king's head crown was toppling:
O Master, so… we were not then led by You,
our struggles were useless, victories… nothing!
O moth, how strong and great you've become
worshipping your flame…this your fate, being
to quickly live then die… and yet you can bear
those burning sparks and despair be scorning…
because you know, fluttering nearer to the fire,
in death you will with your desire, be uniting!
O cruel Love, when on the Day of Judgement
your tyranny the Almighty will be repaying…
and all that blameless blood that you've shed
shall on your haughty head revenge be taking;
place of judgement shall be black, and no less
than Kerbala's wilderness we're still cursing.
So O Judge, perhaps you will show kindness,
and in Your heart pity for sinners be finding…
and think about the memory of their disgrace;
how, dark humiliation their face is staining…

shame stinging and goading them... to repent:
will these not sufficient punishment be giving?
Within the desert of a world gone astray how
many weary wanderers their way were losing!
Love, with beckoning hand, appears to bless,
through the wilderness a way them is finding;
and though like Majnun in the wild they roam
through toils and trials them, home is leading.

*Note: Kerbala... Husain, the son of Ali, the first Imam of Shi'ite Islam, and his followers were treacherously killed at Kerbala by the Caliph's troops, who feared Husain as the new Imam.

Our pathways never led to attainment's garden and our hungry
eyes never fed on Your blessed face... not once it, did we see!
And... as my tears fell like flooding rain and as I sighed
and as I thought then of all of my unsatisfied desires... memory
in vain regret, summoned up that garden where we met,
but... where we now meet no more, I tell this heart with agony.
What have I to do with high estate? I lay fortune down
and everything in the world they take as worthwhile to be...
and... during this day of my humility so precious to me
as is the wine of sovereigns, my cup of fate I now hold tightly.
Do not despair, O Makhfi, although no grass appears
within this desert that is watered by your tears flowing nightly.
Why, with all their arguing, do learned men question
God when He shows His infinite compassion... His mercy?

My garden's green, that is by my tears watered,
and through my soul the rose's perfume kindled
this heart of mine with all its enchanting ways:
Winebringer, bring the cup, for there's appeared
shining within the garden, throughout the night,
a radiance so bright our feast will be illumined...
what is the brilliance through the dark shining?
Heart's blood glowing to heavenly light yielded.
O yes, I've drunk my cup of grief that I cherish,
and loved torment of my heart that is wounded;
and as the scars heal I'm tearing their lips apart
and in my suffering I find relief as I've repented.
So why should I be permitting the winds of care
ruffle my soul like this, like breeze spring stirred,
through the Beloved long, curling, hair seducing?
I rose to be fortunate from despair, has occurred!
O do not fear... for if within the house of prayer
the flickering camphor candle failed and it died,
out from flaming furnace of these sighs of mine
another light will rise, more fierce and illumined.
The fragrant breezes that with the dawn rises...
have not they, Makhfi, taken your soul... it, led

away and drenched it with joy... so all the days
is clinging about you wafts from Paradise's bed?

Ah, for my love's madness, all the world on me scorn is heaping;
so, from its ways I flee… a refuge from its cruelty, to be finding!
Some secluded nest with peace to bless my soul, here in a corner of the wilderness, unseen by worldly eyes, I'll be owning.
Who's the man who's boasting to be love's slave and yet his petty life would save? Poor Love, whose slave's some weakling!
When young I asked, Love denied: what falls, wanderings on Love's road I did… until I brought Wisdom, to me be helping!
Mirror of my heart I brightly polish until for my delight beautifully reflected is the Self's loveliness… these eyes greeting.
Like Jacob, blinded by his agony, no face in all the world is anything to me… what use eyes, except on You to be looking?

Burning heart, how long can you keep hidden, see… flames flare

and smoke from your sighs even the stars in the sky make disappear.

Driven by love I must wander like Majnun where desert's dust falls on tired head, eternally for Layla to cry many a tear.

Soul enlightened by Love never fears a blind world saying, mad to tread Love's ways: joyful, wise, that one's vision's clear.

Makhfi, see how cruel Love is, how proudly it rides above all our hearts, how many a lovers blood… its sword does smear!

When I see the garden in spring, like nightingale rejoicing I'm singing…
if cruel gardener with his wiles tries to trap me, like rose I am smiling.
Morning breeze from garden comes giving no joy to my eyes, for that useless breeze never to me a waft of Your garment is bringing.
Here at garden gate, I wait… why think myself unfortunate? By Your sacred threshold I'll stay, dust with lashes away be sweeping.
Your net has taken bird, my heart, fluttering uselessly; but… though it is Your captive, how from breast can You, sighs be stopping?
O rare, precious Phoenix of the soul I sought You in vain, as my heart wildly longed for You, Your wings above this soul's imagining.
Enemy, keeping me from my quest, even if You enter the sea when from my anger You flee, my burning soul will You… be finding.
O nightingale joyful in the garden, sing; Makhfi won spring in your heart blooming, but in her own autumn's barren winds are moaning.

Love, tell me what Your nature is, so from my kingdom of pride
You can ravish my soul, hold it, keep it as a slave by Your side?
Who knows Your infinite wisdom, what Your lovers bear
when the world proclaims them 'crazy'… derides them as 'wild'?
I'm thirsting to drink my blood, to like sea shed it away,
to sacrifice all I'm seeking to perish as a victim for You, satisfied.
Heart, through pain of loving swooned under grief's load;
O music, come with your magic and relieve my spirit, me guide.
Like Jacob* I sit in ashes overwhelmed by the sky's wrath,
yet from the night of my grief my hope, like dawning will rise.
To bleak mountains like Farhad,* with desire and despair,
I wandered with pain and desire, hope and agony… deep inside.
Makhfi, your secret's unveiled, desire is told everywhere:
who didn't see Joseph's beauty when sold in that market, outside?

*Notes: Jacob... the father of Joseph. The tragic love story of Farhad and Shirin has been told in verse by many master poets of Persia, Nizami's being a masterpiece and the most popular. Shirin (meaning 'sweet') was married to King Khosrau and Farhad, a famous sculptor, had fallen in love with her. The king said he could have her if he cut a passage through a mountain (thinking it to be an impossible task). Farhad worked for many years inspired by his love and eventually succeeded. The king on hearing this sent a messenger to tell him a lie... that Shirin had killed herself. On hearing this he threw himself off the mountain. On finding out this Shirin too committed suicide.

I don't need wine, to me the mesmerising, magic scents caress
breathed by all the garden's flowers, offer a more divine drunkenness.
I pray, forgive me that at the gathering I drank no wine,
I drank a drink more divine, its fragrance day and night I possess.
My heart seems like a bird never joyfully to soar or sing;
as shut in its cage of woe, only in a dream is its garden of happiness.
Why shouldn't I complain as each atom of my body cries
at your tyranny, cruel skies, that on me dark painful days impress?
O Fate, grant me this favour, a little day of joy, of spring,
in cage my heart sings… happy as a bird: death is soon, I stress.
Though I seem so poor, don't pity me for my empty hands,
I still possess my proud eagle soul and have courage under duress!
How many, O many years in prison walls of lonely sorrow
will I stay… not knowing relief, like Jacob blinded by tears: useless?*

Although my proud soul's torn from saddle, thrown in dust by Fate's cruel hands I know my feet the goal will reach, to possess!

Like Love' pilgrims, through desert of life's feast, Makhfi, your pride guide all to Love's realm; feet, like bell through wilderness.

*Note: In Islamic tradition Jacob became blind by weeping for loss of his son Joseph who had been sold by his brothers as a slave into Egypt: he regained his sight on smelling his son's garment returned to him.

Uselessly and long I struggled with you, O enemy: from fight nothing
I won... I guard my treacherous heart, forever from you I am turning.
Is it a wonder if fire in me flares, leaping higher and faster...
and heavy smoke of my sighs into heaven's darkened eyes is drifting?
Though at feast I sit no more, don't think I'm done with joy,
dream I once had is cherished: like wine its memory in veins flowing!
Though in this valley of despair I find no relief from sorrow,
may I have due to prayers a day of rest, a night... peacefully passing!
My fate is sad: I work and am longing until I tire and faint:
still, I can't clean stains... the rust that my desire's mirror is dimming.
Though poor I'm weak too, not daring to use my strong will
to untie purse holding my treasure, golden harvest in lap be spilling!
Yet, Makhfi, if you saw with eyes clean of world's illusion,
look... dervish's rags will be more regal than king's majestic clothing.

My impatient hands from haste couldn't untie the knot of fate...
it is useless to wail about my life laid waste, all my hours unfortunate!
It's strange, in heart my desire's sweet tormenting flame is quenched: impatiently I tore away brands and fire I did cremate.
Never blossoms of success in hope's magic garden were blooming, and my beacon light of happiness gloom does checkmate!
Faithless Beloved, many loved You... many You loved: they give hearts... why care for mine? You need, to me cultivate?

O rival, do not steal from my lips cup holding wine of my delight…

my joy's mirror turns cold and gray, darkening before my sight.

Like the radiant sun banishes gloom, brightening world, I shine with love's oil rust from off my heart with all my might.

Vainly I stretch my imploring hands to hope's garment brightly flying by; though desire dies, hope lives, never trite.

As on cup of last night's feast divine drink held dawn's light falls… night's joy, wine's magic is felt as cup is in sight.

O Farhad, alone, toiling on mountain I've been like you but, not drank sherbet of success, Shirin's sweet lips of delight!

We're dust O Makhfi, this world we trust is worthless: dust's rank of kings, pride in birth, yes you are but dust, outright!

In the dust, in disgrace, is my honour... for the world to see...
why bear shame on my face, what is world's honour to me?
Though my sad head burdens almost unbearable these times heap I don't weep, I smile, on brow no line there be!
Many years grief's with me yet I do not complain, but wage war against despair: it runs, I'm today's Rustom* obviously.
Though Fate to me is cruel, heavenly breezes bring me what I like Jacob seek... scent of garments of Beloved, compassionately.

*Note: Rustom, the son of Zal was the hero of Firdausi's Shahnama, Iran's national epic.

Winebringer hurry, bring wine that my dead heart may be enlivening,
and to withered roses comes like a shower that resurrects spring.
What weary days are these... never the nightingale sings
among cypresses, only morning breeze enters, with roses playing.
Messiah, you can heal O wise Physician, hear our heart!
Give bitter cure, grant relief; don't blame us for from cup shrinking!
O pearly dawn don't glow, don't let night's veil yet go...
I long to sigh arrows into skies, eagerly, before night is leaving.
I crave relief from woes that burn, pains that never end;
all cries are empty breath, not even death at last, soul is relieving!
If on Judgement Day from grief for sins I pray for mercy
for evil done, Perfect One, grant my tears sins away be washing.
O Makhfi, for your fate don't be fearful, don't be upset;
higher on Final Day than king is dervish: none low, none king.

Beloved, don't give me angry looks from your narcissus eyes,
already conquered by your sorcery at your feet my heart lies.
Knots in my heart chords that answered to your touch:
my heart-strings thrill when you're near... so many my sighs.
You sleeping in peace don't know troubles love sends,
or days whose trials and weary nights never end, only arise.
So, where is Mecca? Here is the arch, where I pray...
tell me cure for my sickness, grief's balm everywhere lies.
Love, where do you lead, where does our caravan go?
By Hijaz* desert, longest journey since the world did arise!
My fate's poor, Love never secrets told like to those,
high, fortunate... who near your inner shrine stay, I emphasize!

*Note: Hijaz is the greatest desert in Arabia, along it was passing the main caravan routes.

Why only pray in the mosque, only with friends for wine be calling?
I give up hypocrisy, I always pray: divine cup I am always drinking.

Soul's fountain is dry, my sorrows in my tears don't flow: heart that cried is now mute, in garden nightingale is not singing.

As we tread pilgrims way, torch of inspiration is like fire: dull, blind men don't see it, for desire's cloak they are not longing.

All upon Creation's Day were appointed their fair share: why from destiny more joy, less pain than others are you demanding?

Makhfi, all come for your counsel, their secrets you keep: why you who for them don't tell, your heart's secrets are bearing?

O tormentor, how long on this soul in pain will you be vengeful?
I'd in peace have Love, your poisoned sting to me not hurtful.
No salve soothes heart, lancet's healing pain I crave:
with sharp pain I tear at scars; be kind, cruel, to me be helpful!
From me heart's ripped; ah, let it go, why should I cry?
Over his empty hut the dervish left not one guard to be watchful!
Time of parting sounds, O Makhfi… how long at fire,
shall your infidel soul be blown like a flame, from desire full!

O soul, how hard it is to read life's riddle, beyond and here too,
as in pearl hole without diamond needle-point a piercing to do.
Don't complain that to roses nightingale's wildly singing:
its passion and delight are ours as we garden paths walk through.
By pain made brave we don't seek despair, nor hope, neither last: we take Fate's gift, unlike Zulaikha:* the past we eschew!
O careless ones, vainly your lives treasures passed away,
unaware no years remain talking like tomorrow's child do you.
Worthless is crying tears, grief is fruitless, remorse late:
threshold your lashes sweep, Makhfi? Shrine's desolate, too!

*Note: Zulaikha was the wife of Potiphar. She fell in love with the handsome and enlightened Joseph and could not contain her great love for him. The story of their love was told by many Persian, poets. Jami's version is the best and most famous.

You with such black curls, eyes that take our breath away...
O you with that questioning look, that is leading us astray.
Your eyes that pierce like some blood-stained sword are withdrawn... those eyes, that dagger-like lashes display.
Fanatic you're wrong, paradise is here! Friends, those promising any afterlife forget, get drunk with us here, today!
Forget path to *Kaaba*, the heart is the sacred place... it is time to give away one's life, God is here, now, I say!
O face, excruciatingly beautiful, light never ceasing! It is here, right now, that I am enthralled... never go away!
One cannot find any book on this subject, anywhere; it's only when I look at you I know... that you I can portray!
You want to give your beauty to God, give Makhfi a taste first, for waiting for bit she's here, and will stay!

When You unveil Your fair face, my lashes are burnt by
Your lightning glance… and all night I passionately cry,
while over my heart storms of longing sweep and if I
don't see it, desire it, darkened by an unlit lamp… am I.
I have no hope, none at all, and no comfort anywhere;
by flowing curls of Your hair I am caught… high and dry!
No flower can ever be opening in my bed of flowers…
until all of the blood of my heart, red… its petals does dye.
Sing of your love softly, or let it be, O Makhfi, or the
Hunter will come secretly… hear your voice, you then tie!

The nightingale sings of loving You, moth burns its silken wings Your love drew to fire: see, Your desire's wine, on cups lips clinging!

No ease anywhere now for me, for in the snare... blindly or willingly I fall, no freedom at all I have, Your hair... me, is chaining!

Such tears my eyes cried, blood heart bled: now eyes can't weep, nor failing fountains pour... as dry is source of their feeding.

You, Makhfi, in fire of love, unsatisfied desire, regretfully stay: Love's secrets you told... a bit, so you'll painfully be paying!

Moth, not fierce enough are flames burning your wings of yearning,
and not bright enough is love's torch… in our palace halls shining.

My eyes scattered pearls of tears gaining no consolation;
the matchless jewel of my soul is given away… and all is nothing!

My bitter tale of grief of separation from Friend is long…
it's still unfinished, even though my life its end is finally reaching.

Winebringer, your cup is useless, comforting wine is not mine, drinking alone blood's wine… to others, remedy be giving.

Tale after tale of love is told, liked together like a chain:
chains hold this heavy heart, of freedom… in vain I am dreaming.

Under angry storms of death my life's boat sunk deep;
house did fall, around its dust annihilation's winds are sweeping!

Yet, Makhfi, if in your heart flame of divine love rises,
the lonely desert will be as fair as in Paradise gardens growing.

If from spot on my heart veil falls and the world knows my story...
would roses burn, with an envious light, as they burn... less brightly?

All day, leaping fire of sighs from fast-burning heart rises,
winds of fate blow, scatter it so that my torch isn't yet lit, unfortunately.

I've the world and to wild I fly, but there I'm still hunted:
I seek the quiet of lake and hill but Love still pursues me, unceasingly.

Love's sickness turns my brain, my whole life's so painful:
so, why should I try to flee from grief for it to me is family, obviously!

Here is woe's home, the silent, desolate grief I possess...
how can shining love remain in here in house of pain, tell me!

See my black book's pages... blotted black with sin, strife:
as if the sorrow of all the whole world should pursue me... eternally.

O Makhfi, from this cup's no exultation, nor pain's relief,
for bloody tears flowing from dimming eyes fill it to brim, completely.

You never bring long-lost happiness to quiet my heart's distress...

I crave remedy: why to the crowd should I tell aloud my sadness

that draws scorn upon my name to tell my shame to all?

If in close darkness of the night no light shines... I have stress?

Though for me no torches flare, this grieving heart sees, illuminated by flames of sorrow it keeps bearing... while conscious.

Unsatisfied heart, why tangled in care of worldly hopes will you be restless, seeking those things you will never possess?

You are asking for help in vain from worthless friends... while far up in the skies the Phoenix is flying... without stress.

O see, no sweet herb has grown, because we have only sown in far away springs the seeds of our disgrace... no less.

How could we bear to face the fateful Judgement Day: did not we bring Idol, witnessing that by infidelity we confess

our worship which we, as true believers, keep on living?
On sea of bliss is set our boat, but still is not what we possess.
Over soul the waves of the storm rise, menacing skies: ah no… Makhfi, are your eyes still filling with tears of distress…
and still, this world appears dark: neither can they tell through grief or tired from watching, rose from thorn's sharpness.

O Perfect One, give to Your faithful ones their heart's desires,
on us sad, over-burdened, don't send Your consuming fires!
I can no longer bear the separation and bitter sorrow;
I'm sick, give soul relief: I'm broken, my despair is all sighs!
You we praise: don't tyrannise us, give slave freedom
like Joseph, Canaan's moon, from well You made to rise.
My tears cease, spring feeding their fountains is dry:
O Lord give peace... I'm only a handful of sick dust, I realise.
Return hope's roses to bloom in my desire's garden...
from fire God can burn tulips like torches, after they arise!

On my tormented heart is another deep, glowing stain...
again dawns my day of tears... I'm miserable, in pain!
Much blood I've shed, such long journeys done,
so difficult the path I tread to catch sun's coat's train.
New balm heart bears, new lightning eye has...
why, anger, scorn... your narcissus eyes flashes contain?
From my heart you tore life, it from its place you then ravished, I pray... lift veil hiding your face, again!

I'm long denied vision of Your face, for it, dark, musky hair is covering
like curtain enclosing Kaaba, and unsatisfied hearts it are not seeing.
Reason, speeding runners in desire's valley, we need you not:
we've cure for tiredness, thorns are salves for our pain we are needing.
Each long night alone in my grief remembering You, tears fell:
I, seeking freedom, broke bleeding nails, never fate's knot was untying!
See feast, what better giving guest than wine, music, a party?
Of wines, best… wine of tears; one sad song led to continual singing!
O happy lover you'll get success, walking tall, shadow greater than Jamshid's;* plumes as bright as Huma's,* soul arrogantly soaring.
Crucified by grief a believer lost life for You, yet I have more:
this new joy given me even companions couldn't know, or be gaining.
Rosy faces, like tulip red from tears, displays hearts' dreams:
my tears wash continually the magic cup where the world is appearing.

My love grows, bearing grief for You... proud, patient is my heart like bird, trying to make cage a garden, though useless knowing.

Love's path seems endless, Makhfi; but stride its hard way, don't look back: Temple to bow, fair Idol of dreams you'll be finding!

*Notes: Jamshid was the legendary king of ancient Persia who had a magic cup in which one could see all the world (see two couplets on).
Huma: A symbol, like the Phoenix, for the Beyond State of God.

My way to travel is not that of joy and ease... mine is
that of shame and madness, which I choose, my bliss!
And from my heart such streams of blood will pour on
Judgement Day, desert will be red... a metamorphosis
that will make all of the rosy hues of heaven look pale,
Paradise, in envy of its flaming dye... will darkly hiss!
If being sorry I shed a tear of shame, then I'll be clean
of mistakes, sins, for which my name They'll dismiss!
For God will show compassion upon that Day, when
the record of my transgressions finally wiped away is.
Tree of the world's desire has deeply planted its roots
in the darkness... with sin and shame its bitter fruits.
So, do not barter the wealth that contentment brings:
for lands of a thousand mighty kings, don't give this!
If from heart I let loose many sighs that are so heavy,
dark, blinding, whirling dust from the desert rising is.
Though O Makhfi, God in the end will pardon you...
hem of skirt of Intercession, in fingers hold, and kiss!

Friends help me, or in my madness His secrets to all I may
show:
bearing a stony heart I melt in Love's flame... mocking its
glow.
I descended into death, sky showering cruel blows, pity me
Chosen of God! Enemy when do I rest, how long feel rod's
blow?
My fame's dark: a philanderer, in market... pockets empty:
a dervish, I can give no more... no king with name, glory on
show!
Life's boat sunk: in despair's sea left for shore and Beloved.
I dare go no more, I bow to Fate, turn from care... I scheme?
No!
Spring's passed, rose-leaves scatter, nightingales are silent.
Madness, how long hold my heart? Joy, how long, then you
go?
Life's treasure's uselessly spent, bitterly away from Friend!
Surely, cruel Fate, might end my grief, pain, weariness and
woe?
O king, teacher, see even Alexander's fate, a 'lucky man':
read of Dara,* broken, dejected: both a dark story, blow by
blow!

Festival day, joyfully friends meet; but Makhfi in grief's lane goes on sad feet, no rest or peace: way, dervish does know.

*Note: In Persian poetry Alexander is seen as fortunate, although he missed out on finding the 'Water of Life' (Immortality) in the 'Land of Darkness' (North India) and the enemy he defeated, Dara (or Darius) is seen as unfortunate. Here our poet sees them both as fated. Perhaps she is alluding to Dara Shikoh... see introduction.

Into garden wafts wandering breeze, to tell roses waiting there patiently
You've come: soft, sweet petals open as they kiss Your feet… reverently.
If veil rises from Your face, Joseph won't turn homesick eyes to Caanan, will only see Your face, and offer love to You… only.
No remedy heals heart's distress, but vision of Your beauty.
Here's help, O souls in agony! Don't at tear any wounds… unnecessarily.
It's difficult to find hunted deer, though scent's on the wind; hard to find You… yet hair breathes Khutan's musk in wild, effortlessly!
O happy Makhfi, your day's lucky for at Beloved's feet You can lay your song in homage; happier if you sing in rapture… endlessly!

Your eyes are so tyrannical even morning breeze is hot with anger...
in its breath is no soft appeasement, it only faints, lives no longer!
Like Khizer, strong, youthful, soul steeped in Life's Water,
that Fountain you will be worshipping, with holy words of prayer.
Born into caliph's place, no other bred to such high estate,
you've beauty that is quite divine, than of Paradise's *pari** fairer!
From hope I left hate, false hopes no longer coddling me...
I know that cruel fate has conspired with you, to my fate impair.
Makhfi, your life races, days from your hand fall, forever:
turn no tired traveller from your door... give to each, your cheer!

* Note: A pari is a handsome male inhabitant of Paradise and a huri is a beautiful female inhabitant.

How long of wine, wine cup and wine flagon song be repeating?
How long be renewing the praises of the drinkers and drinking?
Wine and frenzy drenched, wild heart hears no reason:
O my heart, it's much wiser the bowl with tears to be filling!
Ah me, my robe's dirtied, the stain none can remove.
Although my tears in rivers lather it, its useless: not disappearing!
So come, uncork the bottle and fill with wine the cup,
until dreams of blissful union is in rose-perfume soul bathing.
Except by wine awakening heart can know no desire.
Get up... go to winehouse, and there let old wine be flowing.

Don't let your curl's beauty, sending all crazy, bring new
agony
to your lovers: free, wind-tossed, so all see and fall to its
sorcery!
Do not let your love's valley be a place of bitter torment
for sad souls, worn by penance borne... betrayed by love,
already!
No flower, no nightingale am I: from garden I go sadly.
Breeze stay, to that one's garden find a way to greet for
me.
Driven from you I go, patiently like reed I bend, shake
as I take despair's road... for your sake I'm leaving my
body!
Before knowing soul, silence: in desert, he learnt all.*
Don't wake afflicted with poison arrows in his heart,
treacherously.

*Note: The Prophet, Mohammed, who was illiterate, but composed the Koran, that was written down by others.

I'd have as *kohl* for eyes, dust that on your happy doorstep is lying...

and I'd kneel in wait, at last to kiss feet, like angels by... are fluttering!

My soul has suffering girding it and wears it like a garment a king gives to his faithful servant, with pride that one he is out-fitting!

O enemy, waiting by my side, how long must I bend before your rod, to walk pain's path that my friends also have been treading?

Storm sweeps my house, ramparts fail... deep foundations sway: I'm a bird, flying home to stay, finding nest water is overwhelming.

Do not ever be selling the jewel of one's soul, so cheaply, because no friends can help your heart... its wealth to be keeping!

King of the roses, You be kind to the nightingale whose worried mind makes a dervish mad from loving You, for king

riding in majesty won't stop for a mad dervish. Makhfi's blessed: God gave poetry's pearl, divine song... beyond favouring!

All my veins are on fire with the molten rays of Your beauty,
Your love's infused like marrow and life in my bones, completely!
Bold as the Huma my muse on adventurous wings soars into the blue and is poised in the sky for me to see!
Don't hold me low in your esteem, Heaven's secrets flow freely from these lips... when they open to sing, passionately.
Why should I try for fame, struggle for any glory too, I who've scarcely a name and in world is no mark of me?
I stand in life's halls like a motionless statue am I... love of the 'Yes' and the 'No' is my home's lamp, in obscurity.
Trade of the poet's slack as is the market of science: here in my coffers the world's wealth's only nothing, obviously.
Listen to nightingale singing in the garden, Makhfi, its passionate song is an echo of your songs, of your poetry.

Raise the veil hiding Your splendour, moon of all fair and sweet
until the sun, ashamed, vanquished, bows head on Your feet.
Gracious God, how can I live condemned to lonely woe:
grief prevails with moans and wails, courage fails... foes replete.
This is my worship's reward, to spend all life in sighing;
tears unending, woes increasing, burning heart, mind in retreat.
Yet, if fate crowns my hopes, for as long as life remains
every day that brings sun again, makes a year of pain... obsolete!

Noah... O chosen of God, upon the raging ocean floating,

how long sail your ark to where not a landmark is showing?

So precious is what you carry, life is O so precious

you must know: steer carefully so them you're not risking.

Over the boundless ocean you watch and... see in

far off, from the sea, like fleck of foam His hand... rising!

You too, Mohammed, Apostle, Lord of existence,

you whose command over the world and all in it is prevailing.

King of speech and Book... whose complete vision

makes the world be small in the prospect of aeons coming...

regent of all, on floor of whose palace doors angels

understand it as a favour to sit, humbly your word attending.

You, whose unlimited grace... unlimited pardon to

criminal and rend, now to slaves of your house are giving...

on chart of whose perception tells futility's secrets:
destiny dumbly concurring, its immutable seal was
setting.

Who will approach or attend you, whose Ascension
measured the Heavens, while Gabriel... was vainly
following?

Fed by wealth of your mercy earth pours abundantly
its fruitful plains and scents of Paradise, in bowers
breathing.

Majnun's path of love with bare earth as my bed,
it's all the same to me
as many a silken pillow, propped under my head…
it's all the same to me!
Many a bitter drink is mine as I pine away alone:
whether sweet or bitter, poison… or wine instead,
it's all the same to me.
Majnun left home, into desert wastes to roam…
a tiled roof or the heavenly dome over my head…
it's all the same to me.
Wine flow, tears rain, only love can stop my pain:
wine and tears are the same, let it again be said…
it's all the same to me!
Give me the wild to stay, or, Oxus River all day,
the sun-scorched sands or the valley outspread…
it's all the same to me!

In my breast an endless agony hurts... on my heart, is great pain;
and in eyes that are welling up from my heart, crimson tears rain.
All my limbs from head to toe ache with wounds from grief,
no doctor's skill can stitch such wounds to make me whole again.
I fell into love's trap... yet I'm free, one of the dervish band;
and although my back's bent, in the shadow of cypress tall I remain.
If You were angry with me today the passing pain's passed:
tomorrow love will bind us fast and to soothe You I will not abstain.
My life is Yours and my heart's dove I'll slay for Your feast,
and all I have I'll prepare and set it on Love's table... You, to entertain.
Morning to evening my burning soul will flame into the sky,
like a fiery banner on high wave over the world... its mystical slogan!

By *Sweetheart's* poignant glances and by that curling

hair that snares… by eyebrows lances, by eyes bewitching

I swear… with those charms I have been killed: prostrated in the dust… that one, me has been laying!

By white rose of that face… by the black night of that one hair and by the chains of those curls surrounding

and by my heart's suspense I swear that in the dust I'm lying… and now my only cure is to be dying!

By those darkening eyes that hatches raids and ravishment in their lair: by that Hindu-beauty's lashing,

by those pouting lips I swear… that such cruelty consumes me, into everlasting torture me they're dooming!

By that intelligence that gleams and flashes and by lustre of those pearls, and by arrows of lashes whipping,

and… by those curls that me are catching… I'm
now a captive, that those lips with honey me are
baiting.

By those cheeks of pale porcelain… by your pure
moon-like beauty, and by the souls that Love is
hindering:

by those slain by it… you I beg to come, fill my
with joy… me from all this grief and madness be
rescuing.

By magic of braided hair… by your Tartar musk,
by art of your caresses… by your eyebrows line,
arching:

always hoping, always weeping, and sighing…
always longing for those two lips of yours I am
dying.

By highest splendour of Heaven… by infinity
of all the heaven's, by Truth and its Defender
defending…

by the lamp of Prophecy… poor, at your feet I
kneel, one kindly look my way… complete my
healing!

Devotion's flame is weak when the disciple's full of sorrow...
overcome with emotion's the heart that happily does go.
You who in prayer are kneeling at Divine threshold,
reach out your hands and ask... then the benefit will show.
You, who mistakenly complain, life swiftly passes...
let desires die... you gain Life, that death will never overthrow!
If you'd taste Life's Fountain Khizer will guide you
over desert and mountain, ask for the blessed cup to flow.
You've roamed in garden, sore feet, lost in the night;
turn to Gardener for pardon, to lead in light to Him go.
Makhfi, aims you nourish fade in noon of laziness...
drench them with tears, they flourish... increase and grow.

The nightingales are all wailing and crying in each bush tonight…
and my heart in its despair, is sighing for daybreak and light.
Fate, full of ongoing malice like day follows day, takes care to mix for me to drink the cup of pain and despair, outright.
The moth in the flame's dying… candle wastes away: world is full of sighing, hearts are full of pain day and night.
Like Jacob I grieve, no sign of Joseph comes from wild: heart of the parent is broken and careless is the child's plight.
Powers in league to destroy me are subtle… different; where I turn they pursue me, nowhere can I be out of sight.
Oppressor's hand on my shoulder's heavy, I'm spent: how long will I languish and whither in a prison, held tight.
Tyrants, it's said: "Beware of wail of the oppressed!"
Shaft of cry of the persecuted will piece your armour's might!

In the world, not to merit or virtue honours are given; the wealthy distinction inherit, and honours are sold overnight.

Is not it the time for Your long sleep to end,
veil hiding You from our sight, to suspend?
See how the world is wasting from decay...
away all these sickening influences... send?
Let loyalty once again in honour be staying
or from this code of life make real faith end.
The world is full of men fawning and lying,
sweep out all hypocrisy, its reign... amend!
From pole to pole injustice rules the roost,
crush oppressors... their army useless rend.
Justice dressed me with the cloak of night,
let mercy lift cloak and to me sight extend.
Anoint my eyes with grace, tell them look
boldly, undazzled, on Your glory... Friend!
These eyes, Like Jacob's, on road are fixed;
breeze with its healing scent, them, mend.

See, the springtime is over, the nightingale its haunts is fleeing...
still, rosebush stretches longing hands, to catch breezes blowing.
Morning breeze that in days of old from Egyptian skies brought scent of Joseph's robe, light to Jacob's eyes was bringing.
Here no Jacob waits Your healing presence, but sad rose nightingale's absence and petals torn and soiled... keeps mourning.
The songs of toasting and the mourners dirge are stilled: I alone of the gathering, to weep and wail, am now here remaining.
All my treasures have now gone, by robbers stolen away; yet, with my eye upon the lattice, within this house I am staying.
All alone I'm sitting in the darkness of this lonely night, though burning torch of my songs, universe with light are filling.

Yes, I turned back... hard to cross stormy seas and desolate land;
sea had no harbour, upon shore my pony sank leg deep into sand!
I asked for food in every market, none... hunger and despair.
For days I sought Life's Water: I found Khizer, it wasn't at hand!
I sought out sages but no helpful, soothing voice from them:
like Jacob, loneliness without Joseph... left to my tears to it withstand.
Yet, I live, branded by Love, racked by pain I can't disguise;
tears and cries betray my guarded secret, they me as I am... brand!
My star at birth doomed me, or why does heaven curse me?
God's rain of mercy's elsewhere as unworthy I, sink into the sand.
At last, totally exhausted, I seek a salve to ease this pain...
Mohammed, world guardian, hear: world's wide, wider your command!

Where is a kindred soul who in singing like David will join
me
in psalms to be borne by the wind... to threshold of heaven,
immediately.
Our sighs are all too cold, helplessly they flutter to earth,
when they should be like fire, flames ascending skywards
beseechingly.
Each day goes down into night, and vision of union comes
like a dream in the night, doomed to be broken by dawn...
inevitably.
O to be free from all the weeks and days and their weary
coming and going, like wind to pass into Friend's courts
freely.

You live in grief's house: on earth there's no better spot, be sure...
and silent tears are better than wine a wounded heart... to cure.
Moth, why flutter at lamp's fire that desecrates the night?
Rest here on peaceful moonbeam's light on hut that dreams secure.
And... if you need advice to warm heart and enliven mind,
listen to fulfilling words that friends of our faith, both, will ensure...
"Love and wine, roses, blissful peace," so their conversation
goes, that raises discerning soul... expert in inwardness, to procure.
What if heart's consuming fire burns away its earthly pall?
Won't the lover think it fine to chains that hold desire make insecure?

My vigil all night long I keep, through a night with no tomorrow...

my sighs are cold and barren, and never ending is this sorrow!

From my crimson eyes, pearl-drop tears keep flowing...

my heart's a crimson ocean with pearls like rubies I let go.

You are vain, proud, careless, while people bleed under

Your arrows unceasing: no care for their begging, their woe!

O disappointed minstrel, let us cease all complaints...

that wingless, weak, in a second to earth fall... a mere memento!

I waited at the gate of hope and there found no relief for my pain,
and then like Majnun into the wilderness to crawl, I turned again.
With tearless eyes and bursting heart I dragged tired feet to where the Oxus flows... only with unsatisfied thirst, not to retain.
Awhile ago with painful art to unravel life's tangled thread I tried... but the knots were in my heart, so all work was in vain!
Like Farhad, when my cries of despair fell uselessly, I had to go off with broken heart... after gathering up my load of pain.
Like Humayun* I left my land, chased by relentless foes, and never a happy omen over the cloud of my fate arose, again.
Now I wonder with why the powers governing birth and death sent me to this tired earth; only to be returning, in vain?
Makhfi, stay tonight, where your lamp with others burn, 'til all lamps when day returns fade in light covering the domain.

* *Note: Humayun (1508-56) was the Mughal emperor at the inexperienced age of 22. He lost his Indian lands to Sher Shah Suri... but 15 years later with Persian help he retook them.*

Even if admission is denied you, at the door keep
knocking...
if Friend is cold, criticising you, to Him be more
loving.
Will you ever be a stranger to this Beloved One?
In your heart's centre see Him... all His secrets
manifesting.
The road's rough, goal's far, robbers waiting seek
to steal faith's treasure: I've warned you, be not
boasting!
If changing wheel of fortune's unkind, let it roll:
these days of life don't matter, in pain or mirth,
passing.
Makhfi, if Master Gardener says, "Go away,"
wait outside... drink perfume that over fence is
drifting.

Come, my soul, arrange the banquet, set the candles
immediately;
of those dead and gone, drain a cup or two... to their
memory.
Prize the passing hour... ransack all of life's wealth;
watch, and while nightingales sleep, pluck the roses
constantly.
Like captive do not humbly peck at your lot of grain,
boldly snatch the choicest morsels, from fire of pain,
quickly.
Let no ghostly dread scare you, it is a passing show;
life's hardest trials are mere ripples on a stream, you
see?
Don't point fingers of disdain at the poor and lowly,
far better to take sparks as planets flashing, or not,
suddenly.
Fortune always changes, dread not its good or bad;
all the thorny growth of trouble is a mirage growing
uselessly.
With daring, encounter every misfortune you meet;
fight against all sorrow, of defeat... don't dreaming
be!

That is no soul that only warms up with wine:
the true soul warms up to this fluting of mine.
Cold hearts cling to earth: the living fly up in rapture, "Hail to You!" all voices combine.
One step beyond the world it is known your beggar's cap, as kingly crown will shine.
Road is perilous: goal is far from view. What hand leads me safely down the line?
Bricks fall off life's crumbling towers: ruin is near, but who counts the hours decline?
Though lapped in peace here in India, nearer to *Rai's fair bower is heart of mine!
Cold, foodless, the long night passes. Makhfi, hope on... finally comes your time.

*Note: Rai (Rayy) was an ancient, great, beautiful Persian city just a little south of Tehran, excavated in the 1930's.

Souls that greatly grieve look disdainfully on games and laughter...
theirs is a happiness that surroundings of woe stay lying under.
Live in hope of reunion and although your life be lonely...
you can still live on, even if life to its base may reel and totter!
Adviser, don't criticise my tears that are refreshing dew,
longing's garden is joyful... when it is fed with many a tear.
Banquets have no delight, if Beloved's smile isn't there;
yes, even if the wine-cup is Jam's and the wine is Life's Water!
Makhfi, be patient awhile... endure loneliness knowing
that one who does so, to the end... of joy's reward is the inheritor.

Yours, the gracious dews that make roses and herbs fair and bright…

Yours, the eternal fount of splendour from where suns derive light!

When Your mercy like a river surges from its mighty source, ramparts of rebellion shiver into ruins… in way of its raging might!

Tears rain, sighs surge around Your path in heaven, earth… except for those Your favour shelter, tears and sighs are so slight.

All of the universe about You, is full of life and joyfulness: seas and skies and earth without You are empty… without delight!

We've left behind the regions where earthly sorrows reign: onward march our martyred legions, all pain having taken flight.

Makhfi, sing on, never cease… in the garden of our dream over all change of hymn or psalm rules note of nightingale, tonight!

So as to see Your face, for awhile to bear life's weary load I'm resigned…

I'd much prefer to end it, so hard the shame, grief and strife, I find.

I'm so cold… this feeble frame's so bound by icy wind of fate that if all the world was burning… circling fire would not me unbind.

So bound by chains of despair I think, "Can I ever be free?"

I feel like I wear a collar around my neck, band of slavery, a bind.

I'm foul, soiled with habitual vice, garments dirty, stained: even all Kauther's* waters would not wash me clean, you'd find.

*Note: Kauther is one of the main rivers in Paradise.

Gracefully lifting its head in the world as a rose in the garden,

splendid Love arose to desire and adore... away back then.

Then from space's depths murmur of music heralding,

rolling over earth, echoing tumult of song... again and again.

Rays of Beauty covered mountains' skirts... touching creeks until they leapt like flashes of light from cliffs.

When

the wine-red lips like rosebud, blossomed in laughter,

responsive rubies appeared, cascading from cave and mountain.

While chanting this poem in the garden... O Makhfi,

hyacinth and jonquil in earth's heart at your feet say:

"Amen!"

Mine is pure love that pursues its quest through desert and wilderness:

mine is the lonely cry… Majnun's heart, tears, torn clothes weariness.

Mine is work taking all breath, pain's cry, strife's agony…

life lived longing for death, for more dear than life becomes lifelessness.

Mine is love's wine, deadly… flowing like lava in seething brain, lips still dry: mine is this killer cup, this medicine… poisonous.

Mine is the 'shame' (they say), to love unloved: going on, suffering wrong, until under soil my fame, name, song are nothingness.

O Moon of Love, a night elsewhere is lit by Your radiant face:
Your wine's distilled in tears, sighs: cups are souls, vat is grace.
Looking for You the world is gazing into the firmament, another more subtle sky Your rays fill with joy... beyond space.
Arches where kneel enlightened ones are You eyebrows: in temple, mosque, welfare is asked of You by high and base.
Forgetting self, far from other minds, lover's heart lives apart from this turning world... wild words, actions not commonplace.
Sincerely searching, seeing goal, tireless, desire inspired, that one presses on, higher; eyes full of hope for light, to efface.
That one's path is held towards the unknown land, only craving of You in times of agony, to lean on Your arm... apace.
If You and lover are two, soul that loves must go on in pain or bliss, until You, the goal, is found at end of the staircase.

Why do courtier tulips surround rose? Pour wine, why brain be confusing?

In spring, singing is sweet... where is the host? Why so long in arriving?

Life reflects seasons' flight: winter, spring, summer, autumn... through all, I am happy with wine and song, no one the end is knowing.

Even if we are from nothing, end in nothing... Creator is kind.

Bring red wine, Jamshid's royal cup... sit near stream, wine be drinking!

Doomed from the start... why go on? Ascetic, why fast, pray?

Spring is here, why worry? Give up love, wine? We sin? He's forgiving!

Time's a pageant where some lead, others follow in the dance: all's false, seeming fair; pale lovers wander, happy only by luck happening.

Quiet, whom ecstasy's wine's strange, mystical songs a bore: hermit, dervish, knows no more than us! Sceptic, stop stupid criticising!

Lover hugs fire in heart: drunkard drinks, stops complaining.

Makhfi's laments: monk wants water, Hafiz, wine; is God, forthcoming?

BOOKS PUBLISHED BY NEW HUMANITY BOOKS BOOK HEAVEN

*Most 6" x 9" (15 cm x 23 cm) Paperbacks Perfectbound
unless stated otherwise...
Most also available in pdf format
from: www.newhumanitybooks.com
check out our website for prices & full descriptions of each book.
Also available from Amazon.com
many titles are also in Kindle format e-books*

TRANSLATIONS

(NOTE: All translations by Paul Smith are in clear, modern English and in the correct rhyme-structure of the originals and as close to the true meaning as possible.)

DIVAN OF HAFIZ
Revised Translation & Introduction by Paul Smith
This is a completely revised one volume edition of the only modern, poetic version of Hafiz's masterpiece of 791 *ghazals, masnavis, rubais* and other poems/songs. The spiritual and historical and human content is here in understandable, beautiful poetry: the correct rhyme-structure has been achieved, without intruding, in readable (and singable) English. In the Introduction of 70 pages his life story is told in greater detail than any where else; his spirituality is explored, his influence on the life, poetry and art of the East and the West, the form and function of his poetry, and the use of his book as a worldly guide and spiritual oracle. His Book, like the *I Ching*, is one of the world's Great Oracles. Included are notes to most poems, glossary and selected bibliography and two indexes. First published in a two-volume hardback limited edition in 1986 the book quickly went out of print. 542 pages.

PERSIAN AND HAFIZ SCHOLARS AND ACADEMICS WHO HAVE COMMENTED ON PAUL SMITH'S TRANSLATION OF HAFIZ'S 'DIVAN'.
"It is not a joke... the English version of ALL the *ghazals* of Hafiz is a great feat and of paramount importance. I am astonished. If he comes to Iran I will kiss the fingertips that wrote such a masterpiece inspired by the

Creator of all and I will lay down my head at his feet out of respect." Dr. Mir Mohammad Taghavi (Dr. of Literature) Tehran.

"I have never seen such a good translation and I would like to write a book in Farsi and introduce his Introduction to Iranians." Mr B. Khorramshai, Academy of Philosophy, Tehran.

"Superb translations. 99% Hafiz 1% Paul Smith." Ali Akbar Shapurzman, translator of many mystical works in English to Persian and knower of Hafiz's *Divan* off by heart.

"I was very impressed with the beauty of these books." Dr. R.K. Barz. Faculty of Asian Studies, Australian National University.

"Smith has probably put together the greatest collection of literary facts and history concerning Hafiz." Daniel Ladinsky (Penguin Books author of poems inspired by Hafiz).

HAFIZ – THE ORACLE
(For Lovers, Seekers, Pilgrims, and the God-Intoxicated).
Translation & Introduction by Paul Smith. 441 pages.

HAFIZ OF SHIRAZ.
The Life, Poetry and Times of the Immortal Persian Poet.
In Three Books by Paul Smith. Over 1900 pages, 3 volumes.

PIERCING PEARLS: THE COMPLETE ANTHOLOGY OF PERSIAN POETRY
(Court, Sufi, Dervish, Satirical, Ribald, Prison & Social Poetry from the 9th to the 20th century.) Volume One
Translations, Introduction and Notes by Paul Smith. Pages 528.

PIERCING PEARLS: THE COMPLETE ANTHOLOGY OF PERSIAN POETRY
(Court, Sufi, Dervish, Satirical, Ribald, Prison & Social Poetry from the 9th to the 20th century.) Vol. Two
Translations, Introduction and Notes by Paul Smith. Pages 462.

DIVAN OF SADI: His Mystical Love-Poetry.
Translation & Introduction by Paul Smith. 421 pages.

RUBA'IYAT OF SADI
Translation & Introduction by Paul Smith. 151 pages.

WINE, BLOOD & ROSES:
ANTHOLOGY OF TURKISH POETS
Sufi, Dervish, Divan, Court & Folk Poetry from the 12th – 20th Century
Translations, Introductions, Notes etc., by Paul Smith. Pages 286.

OBEYD ZAKANI: THE DERVISH JOKER.
A Selection of his Poetry, Prose, Satire, Jokes and Ribaldry.
Translation & Introduction by Paul Smith. 305 pages.

OBEYD ZAKANI'S > MOUSE & CAT ^ ^
(The Ultimate Edition)
Translation & Introduction etc by Paul Smith. 191 pages.

THE GHAZAL: A WORLD ANTHOLOGY
Translations, Introductions, Notes, Etc. by Paul Smith. Pages 658.

NIZAMI: THE TREASURY OF MYSTERIES
Translation & Introduction by Paul Smith. 251 pages.

NIZAMI: LAYLA AND MAJNUN
Translation & Introduction by Paul Smith. 215 pages.

UNITY IN DIVERSITY
Anthology of Sufi and Dervish Poets of the Indian Sub-Continent
Translations, Introductions, Notes, Etc. by Paul Smith. Pages… 356.

RUBA'IYAT OF RUMI
Translation & Introduction and Notes by Paul Smith. 367 pages.

THE *MASNAVI*: A WORLD ANTHOLOGY
Translations, Introduction and Notes by Paul Smith. 498 pages.

HAFIZ'S FRIEND, JAHAN KHATUN:
The Persian Princess Dervish Poet…
A Selection of Poems from her *Divan*
Translated by Paul Smith with Rezvaneh Pashai. 267 pages.

PRINCESSES, SUFIS, DERVISHES, MARTYRS & FEMINISTS: NINE GREAT WOMEN POETS OF THE EAST: A Selection of the Poetry of Rabi'a of Basra, Rabi'a of Balkh, Mahsati, Lalla Ded, Jahan Khatun, Makhfi, Tahirah, Hayati and Parvin.
Translation & Introduction by Paul Smith. Pages 367.

RUMI: SELECTED POEMS
Translation, Introduction & Notes by Paul Smith. 220 pages.

KABIR: SEVEN HUNDRED SAYINGS (SAKHIS).
Translation & Introduction by Paul Smith. 190 pages. Third Edition

SHAH LATIF: SELECTED POEMS
Translation & Introduction by Paul Smith. 172 pages

LALLA DED: SELECTED POEMS
Translation & Introduction by Paul Smith. 140 pages.

BULLEH SHAH: SELECTED POEMS
Translation & Introduction by Paul Smith. 141 pages.

NIZAMI: MAXIMS
Translation & Introduction Paul Smith. 214 pages.

KHIDR IN SUFI POETRY: A SELECTION
Translation & Introduction by Paul Smith. 267 pages.

ADAM: THE FIRST PERFECT MASTER AND POET
by Paul Smith. 222 pages.

MODERN SUFI POETRY: A SELECTION
Translations & Introduction by Paul Smith. Pages 249

LIFE, TIMES & POETRY OF NIZAMI
by Paul Smith. 97 pages.

RABI'A OF BASRA: SELECTED POEMS
Translation by Paul Smith. 102 pages.

RABI'A OF BASRA & MANSUR HALLAJ
~Selected Poems~
Translation & Introduction Paul Smith. Pages 134

SATIRICAL PROSE OF OBEYD ZAKANI
Translation and Introduction by Paul Smith. 212 pages.

KHAQANI: SELECTED POEMS
Translation & Introduction by Paul Smith. 197 pages.

IBN 'ARABI: SELECTED POEMS
Translation & Introduction by Paul Smith. 121 pages.

THE *GHAZAL* IN SUFI & DERVISH POETRY:
An Anthology:
Translations, Introductions, by Paul Smith Pages 548.

A GREAT TREASURY OF POEMS
BY GOD-REALIZED & GOD-INTOXICATED POETS
Translation & Introduction by Paul Smith. Pages 804.

MAKHFI: THE PRINCESS SUFI POET ZEB-UN-NISSA
A Selection of Poems from her *Divan*
Translation & Introduction by Paul Smith. 154 pages.

~ THE SUFI RUBA'IYAT ~
A Treasury of Sufi and Dervish Poetry in the *Ruba'i* form,
from Rudaki to the 21st Century
Translations, Introductions, by Paul Smith. Pages… 304.

LOVE'S AGONY & BLISS: ANTHOLOGY OF URDU
POETRY: Sufi, Dervish, Court and Social Poetry
from the 16th - 20th Century
Translations, Introductions, Etc. by Paul Smith. Pages 298.

RUBA'IYAT OF ANSARI
Translation & Introduction by Paul Smith. 183 pages

THE RUBAI'YAT: A WORLD ANTHOLOGY:
Court, Sufi, Dervish, Satirical, Ribald, Prison and Social Poetry in the
Ruba'i form from the 9th to the 20th century from the Arabic, Persian,
Turkish, Urdu and English.
Translations, Introduction and Notes by Paul Smith Pages 388.

BREEZES OF TRUTH
Selected Early & Classical Arabic Sufi Poetry
Translations, Introductions by Paul Smith. Pages 248.

THE~DIVINE~WINE:
A Treasury of Sufi and Dervish Poetry (Volume One)
Translations, Introductions by Paul Smith. Pages… 522.

THE~DIVINE~WINE:
A Treasury of Sufi and Dervish Poetry (Volume Two)
Translations, Introductions by Paul Smith. Pages… 533.

TONGUES ON FIRE: An Anthology of the Sufi, Dervish,
Warrior & Court Poetry of Afghanistan.
Translations, Introductions, Etc. by Paul Smith. 322 pages.

THE SEVEN GOLDEN ODES (QASIDAS) OF ARABIA *(The Mu'allaqat)*
Translations, Introduction & Notes by Paul Smith. Pages… 147.

THE QASIDA: A WORLD ANTHOLOGY
Translations, Introduction & Notes by Paul Smith. Pages… 354.

IBN AL-FARID: WINE & THE MYSTIC'S PROGRESS
Translation, Introduction & Notes by Paul Smith. 174 pages.

RUBA'IYAT OF ABU SA'ID
Translation, Introduction & Notes by Paul Smith. 227 pages.

RUBA'IYAT OF BABA TAHIR
Translations, Introduction & Notes by Paul Smith. 154 pages.

THE POETS OF SHIRAZ
Sufi, Dervish, Court & Satirical Poets from the 9th to the 20th Centuries of the fabled City of Shiraz.
Translations & Introduction & Notes by Paul Smith. 428 pages.

RUBA'IYAT OF 'ATTAR
Translation, Introduction & Notes by Paul Smith. 138 Pages.

RUBA'IYAT OF MAHSATI
Translation, Introduction & Notes by Paul Smith. 150 Pages.

RUBA'IYAT OF JAHAN KHATUN
Translation by Paul Smith with Rezvaneh Pashai
Introduction & Notes by Paul Smith. 157 Pages.

RUBA'IYAT OF SANA'I
Translation, Introduction & Notes by Paul Smith. 129 Pages.

RUBA'IYAT OF JAMI
Translation, Introduction & Notes by Paul Smith. 179 Pages.

RUBA'IYAT OF SARMAD
Translation, Introduction & Notes by Paul Smith. 381 pages.

RUBA'IYAT OF HAFIZ
Translation, Introduction & Notes by Paul Smith. 221 Pages.

GREAT SUFI POETS OF THE PUNJAB & SINDH: AN ANTHOLOGY
Translations & Introductions by Paul Smith 166 pages.

YUNUS EMRE, THE TURKISH DERVISH: SELECTED POEMS
Translation, Introduction & Notes by Paul Smith. Pages 237.

RUBA'IYAT OF KAMAL AD-DIN
Translation, Introduction & Notes by Paul Smith. Pages 170.

RUBA'YAT OF KHAYYAM
Translation, Introduction & Notes by Paul Smith
Reprint of 1909 Introduction by R.A. Nicholson. 268 pages.

RUBA'IYAT OF AUHAD UD-DIN
Translation and Introduction by Paul Smith. 127 pages.

RUBA'IYAT OF AL-MA'ARRI
Translation & Introduction by Paul Smith. 151 pages

ANTHOLOGY OF CLASSICAL ARABIC POETRY
(From Pre-Islamic Times to Al-Shushtari)
Translations, Introduction and Notes by Paul Smith. Pages 287.

THE *QIT'A*
Anthology of the 'Fragment' in Arabic, Persian and Eastern Poetry.
Translations, Introduction and Notes by Paul Smith. Pages 423.

HEARTS WITH WINGS
Anthology of Persian Sufi and Dervish Poetry
Translations, Introductions, Etc., by Paul Smith. Pages 623.

HAFIZ: SELECTED POEMS
Translation, Introduction & Notes by Paul Smith. 227 Pages.

'ATTAR: SELECTED POETRY
Translation, Introduction & Notes by Paul Smith. 222 pages.

SANA'I : SELECTED POEMS
Translation, Introduction & Notes by Paul Smith. 148 Pages.

THE ROSE GARDEN OF MYSTERY: SHABISTARI
Translation by Paul Smith.
Introduction by E.H. Whinfield & Paul Smith. Pages 182.

RUDAKI: SELECTED POEMS
Translation, Introduction & Notes by Paul Smith. 142 pages.

SADI: SELECTED POEMS
Translation, Introduction & Notes by Paul Smith. 207 pages.

JAMI: SELECTED POEMS
Translation, Introduction by Paul Smith. 183 Pages.

NIZAMI: SELECTED POEMS
Translation & Introduction by Paul Smith. 235 pages.

RUBA'IYAT OF BEDIL
Translation & Introduction by Paul Smith. 154 pages.

BEDIL: SELECTED POEMS
Translation & Introduction by Paul Smith. Pages… 147.

ANVARI: SELECTED POEMS
Translation & Introduction by Paul Smith. 164 pages.

RUBA'IYAT OF 'IRAQI
Translation & Introduction by Paul Smith. 138 pages.

THE WISDOM OF IBN YAMIN: SELECTED POEMS
Translation & Introduction Paul Smith. 155 pages.

NESIMI: SELECTED POEMS
Translation & Introduction by Paul Smith. 169 pages.

SHAH NI'TMATULLAH: SELECTED POEMS
Translation & Introduction by Paul Smith. 168 pages.

AMIR KHUSRAU: SELECTED POEMS
Translation & Introduction by Paul Smith. 201 pages.

A WEALTH OF POETS:
Persian Poetry at the Courts of Sultan Mahmud in Ghazneh
& Sultan Sanjar in Ganjeh (998-1158)
Translations, Introduction and Notes by Paul Smith. Pages 264.

SHIMMERING JEWELS: Anthology of Poetry Under the Reigns
of the Mughal Emperors of India (1526-1857)
Translations, Introductions, Etc. by Paul Smith. Pages 463.

RAHMAN BABA: SELECTED POEMS
Translation & Introduction by Paul Smith. 141 pages.

RUBA'IYAT OF DARA SHIKOH
Translation & Introduction by Paul Smith. 148 pages.

ANTHOLOGY OF POETRY OF THE CHISHTI SUFI ORDER
Translations & Introduction by Paul Smith. Pages 313.

POEMS OF MAJNUN
Translation & Introduction by Paul Smith. 220 pages.

RUBA'IYAT OF SHAH NI'MATULLAH
Translation & Introduction by Paul Smith. 125 pages.

ANSARI: SELECTED POEMS
Translation & Introduction by Paul Smith. 156 pages.

BABA FARID: SELECTED POEMS
Translation & Introduction by Paul Smith. 164 pages.

POETS OF THE NI'MATULLAH SUFI ORDER
Translations & Introduction by Paul Smith. 244 pages.

MU'IN UD-DIN CHISHTI: SELECTED POEMS
Translation & Introduction by Paul Smith. 171 pages.

QASIDAH BURDAH:
THE THREE POEMS OF THE PROPHET'S MANTLE
Translations & Introduction by Paul Smith. Pages 116.

KHUSHAL KHAN KHATTAK: THE GREAT POET
& WARRIOR OF AFGHANISTAN, SELECTED POEMS
Translation & Introduction by Paul Smith. Pages 187.

RUBA'IYAT OF ANVARI
Translation & Introduction by Paul Smith. 104 pages.

'IRAQI: SELECTED POEMS
Translation & Introduction by Paul Smith. 156 pages.

MANSUR HALLAJ: SELECTED POEMS
Translation & Introduction by Paul Smith. Pages 178.

RUBA'IYAT OF BABA AFZAL
Translation & Introduction by Paul Smith. 178 pages.

RUMI: SELECTIONS FROM HIS *MASNAVI*
Translation & Introduction by Paul Smith. 260 pages.

WINE OF LOVE: AN ANTHOLOGY,
Wine in the Poetry of Arabia, Persia, Turkey &
the Indian Sub-Continent from Pre-Islamic Times to the Present
Translations & Introduction by Paul Smith. 645 pages.

GHALIB: SELECTED POEMS
Translation & Introduction by Paul Smith. Pages 200.

THE ENLIGHTENED SAYINGS OF HAZRAT 'ALI
The Right Hand of the Prophet
Translation & Introduction by Paul Smith. Pages 260.

HAFIZ: TONGUE OF THE HIDDEN
A Selection of *Ghazals* from his *Divan*
Translation & Introduction Paul Smith. 133 pages. Third Edition.

~ HAFIZ: A DAYBOOK ~
Translation & Introduction by Paul Smith. 375 pages.

~* RUMI* ~ A Daybook
Translation & Introduction by Paul Smith. Pages 383.

SUFI POETRY OF INDIA ~ A Daybook~
Translation & Introduction by Paul Smith. Pages 404.

~ SUFI POETRY~ A Daybook
Translation & Introduction by Paul Smith. Pages 390.

~*KABIR*~ A Daybook
Translation & Introduction by Paul Smith. 382 pages.

~ABU SA'ID & SARMAD~ A Sufi Daybook
Translation & Introduction by Paul Smith. 390 pages.

~*SADI*~ A Daybook
Translation & Introduction by Paul Smith. 394 pages.

NIZAMI, KHAYYAM & 'IRAQI ... A Daybook
Translation & Introduction by Paul Smith. 380 pages.

ARABIC & AFGHAN SUFI POETRY ... A Daybook
Translation & Introduction by Paul Smith. 392 pages.

TURKISH & URDU SUFI POETS... A Daybook
Translation & Introduction by Paul Smith. 394 pages.

SUFI & DERVISH RUBA'IYAT ($9^{th} - 14^{th}$ century)
A DAYBOOK
Translation & Introduction by Paul Smith. 394 pages.

SUFI & DERVISH RUBA'IYAT ($14th^{th} - 20^{th}$ century)
A DAYBOOK
Translation & Introduction by Paul Smith. 394 pages.

~SAYINGS OF THE BUDDHA: A DAYBOOK~
Revised Translation by Paul Smith from F. Max Muller's. 379 pages.

GREAT WOMEN MYSTICAL POETS OF THE EAST
~ A Daybook ~
Translation & Introduction by Paul Smith. 385 pages.

ABU NUWAS SELECTED POEMS
Translation & Introduction by Paul Smith. 154 pages.

HAFIZ: THE SUN OF SHIRAZ:
Essays, Talks, Projects on the Immortal Poet
by Paul Smith. 249 pages.

~*NAZIR AKBARABADI*~ SELECTED POEMS
Translation and Introduction Paul Smith. 191 pages.

~RUBA'IYAT OF IQBAL~
Translation & Introduction by Paul Smith. 175 pages.

~*IQBAL*~ SELECTED POETRY
Translation & Introduction by Paul Smith. 183 pages.

>THE POETRY OF INDIA<
Anthology of Poets of India from 3500 B.C. to the 20th century
Translations, Introductions… Paul Smith. Pages… 622.

BHAKTI POETRY OF INDIA… AN ANTHOLOGY
Translations & Introductions Paul Smith. Pages 236.

SAYINGS OF KRISHNA: A DAYBOOK
Translation & Introduction Paul Smith. Pages 376.

~CLASSIC POETRY OF AZERBAIJAN~ An Anthology~
Translation & Introduction Paul Smith. 231 pages.

THE TAWASIN: MANSUR HALLAJ
(Book of the Purity of the Glory of the One)
Translation & Introduction Paul Smith. Pages 264.

MOHAMMED In Arabic, Sufi & Eastern Poetry
Translation & Introduction by Paul Smith. Pages 245.

GITA GOVINDA
The Dance of Divine Love of Radha & Krishna
>Jayadeva< Translation by Puran Singh & Paul Smith. Pages 107.

GREAT WOMEN MYSTICAL POETS OF THE EAST
~ A Daybook ~ Translation & Introduction by Paul Smith. 385 pages.

~SUFI LOVE POETRY~ An Anthology
Translation & Introduction Paul Smith. Pages 560.

HUMA: SELECTED POEMS OF MEHER BABA
Translation & Introduction Paul Smith. Pages 244.

RIBALD POEMS OF THE SUFI POETS
Abu Nuwas, Sana'i, Anvari, Mahsati, Rumi, Sadi and Obeyd Zakani…
Translation & Introduction Paul Smith. 206 pages.

FIVE GREAT EARLY SUFI MASTER POETS
Mansur Hallaj, Baba Tahir, Abu Sa'id, Ansari & Sana'i
Translation & Introduction by Paul Smith. Pages 617

FIVE GREAT CLASSIC SUFI MASTER POETS
Khaqani, Mu'in ud-din Chishti, 'Attar & Auhad ud-din Kermani
Translation & Introduction Paul Smith. Pages 541.

ANTHOLOGY OF WOMEN MYSTICAL POETS
OF THE MIDDLE-EAST & INDIA
Translation & Introduction Paul Smith. Pages 497.

FOUR MORE GREAT CLASSIC SUFI MASTER POETS
Sadi, 'Iraqi, Yunus Emre, Shabistari.
Translation & Introduction Paul Smith. Pages 562.

~ANOTHER~
FOUR GREAT CLASSIC SUFI MASTER POETS
Amir Khusrau, Ibn Yamin, Hafiz & Nesimi
Translation & Introduction Paul Smith. Pages 636.

FOUR GREAT LATER CLASSIC SUFI MASTER POETS
Shah Ni'mat'ullah, Jami, Dara Shikoh & Makhfi
Translation & Introduction Paul Smith. Pages 526.

THE FOUR LAST GREAT SUFI MASTER POETS
Shah Latif, Nazir Akbarabadi, Ghalib and Iqbal
Translation & Introduction Paul Smith. Pages 616.

'ATTAR & KHAQANI: SUFI POETRY ~A Daybook~
Translation & Introduction Paul Smith. 388 pages.

POET-SAINTS OF MAHARASHTRA:
SELECTED POEMS
Translations & Introductions by Paul Smith. Pages 198.

ABHANGS & BHAJANS OF THE GREATEST INDIAN
POET-SAINTS
Translations & Introductions Paul Smith. Pages 214.

A TREASURY OF LESSER-KNOWN GREAT SUFI POETS
Translation & Introduction Paul Smith. Pages 736.

HATEF OF ISFAHAN AND HIS FAMOUS *TARJI-BAND*
Translation & Introduction Paul Smith. Pages 129.

CLASSIC BATTLE POEMS OF ANCIENT INDIA
& ARABIA, PERSIA & AFGHANISTAN
Translation & Introduction Paul Smith. Pages 246.

~ANOTHER~ FIVE GREAT CLASSIC SUFI MASTER POETS
Ibn al-Farid, Ibn 'Arabi, Baba Farid, Baba Afzal, Rumi.
Translation & Introduction Paul Smith. Pages 626.

ANTHOLOGY OF GREAT SUFI & MYSTICAL
POETS OF PAKISTAN
Translation & Introduction by Paul Smith. Pages 260.

ZARATHUSHTRA: SELECTED POEMS
A New Verse Translation and Introduction by Paul Smith
from the Original Translation by D.J. Irani.
Original Introduction by Rabindranath Tagore. 141 pages.

THE DHAMMAPADA: The Gospel of the Buddha
Revised Version by Paul Smith
from translation from the Pali of F. Max Muller. 247 pages

THE YOGA SUTRAS OF PATANJALI
"The Book of the Spiritual Man" An Interpretation By Charles Johnston,
General Introduction by Paul Smith. Pages 173.

BHAGAVAD GITA: The Gospel of the Lord Shri Krishna
Translated from Sanskrit with Introduction by Shri Purohit Swami,
General Introductions by Charles Johnston, Revised into Modern English
with an Introduction by Paul Smith. 326 pages.

~TAO TE CHING~ by Lao Tzu
Modern English Version by Paul Smith
from the Translation from the Chinese by Paul Carus. Pages 147.

THE PERSIAN ORACLE: Hafiz of Shiraz
Translation, Introduction & Interpretations by Paul Smith
 Pages 441.

CAT & MOUSE: Obeyd Zakani
Translation & Introduction by Paul Smith
Large Format Paperback, 7" x 10" Illustrated 183 pages

HAFEZ: THE DIVAN
Volume One: The Poems
Revised Translation Paul Smith
Large Format Paperback "7 x 10" 578 pages

HAFEZ: THE DIVAN
Volume Two: Introduction
Paul Smith
Large Format Paperback 7" x 10" 224 pages.

~ SAADI ~ THE DIVAN
Revised Translation & Introduction Paul Smith
Large Format Paperback 7" x 10" 548 pages.

HAFEZ: BOOK OF DIVINATION
Translation, Introduction & Interpretations by Paul Smith
Large Format Edition, 7" x 10" 441 pages

LAYLA AND MAJNUN: NIZAMI
Translation & Introduction by Paul Smith
Large Format Edition, 7" x 10" 239 pages.

HAFEZ: DIVAN
Revised Translation, Introduction Etc by Paul Smith
Large Format Edition 7" x 10" 800 pages.

HAFEZ OF SHIRAZ:
The Life, Poetry and Times of the Immortal Persian Poet
Books 1.2 & 3. (The Early Years, The Middle Years, The Later Years)
by Paul Smith
Large Format Edition 7" x 10" over 800 pages each book.

OMAR KHAYYAM: RUBA'IYAT
Translation & Introduction Paul Smith
Reprint of 1909 Introduction by R.A. Nicholson
Large Format Edition, 7" x 10" Illustrated, 280 pages.

ROSE GARDEN OF MYSTERY: SHABISTARI
Translation by Paul Smith.
Introduction by E.H. Whinfield & Paul Smith
Large Format Edition 7" x 10" 182 pages.

SUFIS, PRINCESSES & DERVISHES, MARTYRS &
FEMINISTS: Ten Great Women Poets of the East
Translations & Introductions Paul Smith
Large Format Edition 7" x 10" 410 pages.

ARABIC SUFI POETRY: An Anthology
Translation & Introduction Paul Smith
Large Format Edition 7" x 10" 387 pages.

A QUILT OF WOMEN SPIRITUAL POETS
OF THE MIDDLE-EAST & INDIA
Translation & Introduction Paul Smith
Large Format Edition 7" x 10" 509 pages.

THE BOOK OF ABU SA'ID
Ruba'iyat... Life & Times & Teachings
Translation by Paul Smith
Introduction by Paul Smith & R.A. Nicholson
Large Format Edition 7" x 10" 350 pages.

THE BOOK OF KABIR
Short Poems *(Sakhis)*
Translation & Introduction Paul Smith
Large Format Edition 7" x 10" 698 pages.

~RUMI~ *Ruba'iyat*
Translation & Introduction Paul Smith
Large Format Edition 7" x 10" 368 pages

THE BOOK OF FARID AL-DIN 'ATTAR
Ruba'is, Ghazals & Masnavis
Translation & Introduction Paul Smith
Large Format Edition 7" x 10" 207 pages

THE BOOK OF OBEYD ZAKANI
Poetry, Prose, Satire, Jokes and Ribaldry.
Translation and Introduction by Paul Smith
Large Format Edition 7" x 10" 357 pages.

THE BOOK OF MANSUR HALLAJ
Selected Poems & The Tawasin
Translation & Introduction Paul Smith
Large Format Edition 7" x 10" 323 pages

THE BOOK OF RUMI
Ruba'is, Ghazals, Masnavis and a *Qasida*
Translation & Introduction Paul Smith
Large Format Edition 7" x 10" 476 pages.

THE BOOK OF SARMAD
Translation & Introduction Paul Smith
Large Format Edition 7" x 10" 407 pages

THE BOOK OF IBN AL-FARID
Translation & Introduction Paul Smith
Large Format Edition 7" x 10" 178 pages

THREE SUFI-MARTYR POETS OF INDIA
Sarmad, Dara Shikoh & Makhfi
Translation & Introduction Paul Smith
Large Format Edition 7" x 10" pages 334.

THE BOOK OF KHAQANI
Translation & Introduction by Paul Smith
Large Format Paperback 7' x 10" pages 230

DRUNK ON GOD
Anthology Poems by God-Realized & God-Intoxicated Poets
Translation & Introduction by Paul Smith
Large Format Paperback 7" x 10" pages 804.

POETRY OF INDIA
Anthology of the Greatest Poets of India
Translations, Introductions by Paul Smith
Large Format Paperback 7" x 10" Pages 760

THE BOOK OF JAMI
Translation & Introduction by Paul Smith
Large Format Paperback 7" x 10" pages 233.

THE BOOK OF ANSARI
Translation & Introduction by Paul Smith
Large Format Paperback 7" x 10" pages 231.

YUNUS EMRE & NESIMI:
THE TWO GREAT TURKISH SUFI POETS...
Their Lives & a Selection of their Poems
Translation & Introduction Paul Smith
Large Format Paperback 7" x 10" 416 pages.

THE BOOK OF NESIMI
Translation & Introduction by Paul Smith
Large Format Paperback 7" x 10" pages 250.

THE BOOK OF IQBAL
Translation & Introduction by Paul Smith
Large Format Paperback 7" x 10" pages 252.

THE BOOK OF 'IRAQI
Translation & Introduction by Paul Smith
Large Format Paperback 7" x 10" pages 186.

THE BOOK OF TURKISH POETRY
Anthology of Sufi, Dervish, Divan, Court & Folk Poetry
from the 12th – 20th Century
Translation & Introduction Paul Smith
7" x 10" Large Format Paperback 341 pages

THE BOOK OF HAFIZ (HAFEZ)
Translation, Introduction Etc. Paul Smith
Large Format Edition 7" x 10" 532 pages.

THE BOOK OF SANA'I
Translation & Introduction Paul Smith
Large Format Paperback 167 pages.

THE BOOK OF ECSTASY OR
THE BALL & THE POLO-STICK
by 'Arifi Translation & Introduction Paul Smith
Large Format Paperback 7" x 10" 221 pages.

ANTHOLOGY OF SUFI & FOLK STROPHE POEMS
OF PERSIA AND THE INDIAN SUB-CONTINENT
Translation & Introduction Paul Smith
Large Format Paperback 7" x 10" 423 pages.

THE BOOK OF MAJNUN
Translation & Introduction by Paul Smith
Large Format Paperback 7" x 10" 336 pages.

THE BOOK OF MU'IN UD-DIN CHISHTI
Translation & Introduction Paul Smith
Large Format Paperback 7" x 10" 315 pages.

THE BOOK OF SHAH NI'MAT'ULLAH
Translation & Introduction Paul Smith
Large Format Paperback 7" x 10" 232 pages.

THE BOOK OF NAZIR AKBARABADI
Translation & Introduction Paul Smith
Large Format Paperback 7" x 10" 329 pages.

POETS OF SHIRAZ AT THE TIME OF HAFIZ
Translation & Introduction Paul Smith 455 pages.

THE BIG BOOK OF SUFI POETRY
An Anthology
Translation & Introduction by Paul Smith
Large Format 7" x 10" 798 pages.

THE BIG BOOK OF PERSIAN POETRY: An Anthology
Court, Sufi, Dervish, Satirical, Ribald, Prison and Social Poetry
from the 9th to the 20th century
Translation, Introduction by Paul Smith
Large Format Paperback 7" x 10" 777 pages

THE BOOK OF SHABISTARI
The Rose Garden of Mystery
Translation & Introduction Paul Smith
Large Format Paperback 7" x 10" 261 pages.

THE BOOK OF ABU NUWAS
Translation & Introduction Paul Smith
Large Format Paperback 7" x 10" 196 pages.

THE BOOK OF DARA SHIKOH
Life, Poems & Prose
Large Format Paperback 7" x 10" 276 pages.

BHAGAVAD GITA & GITA GOVINDA
Translation & Introduction Paul Smith
With Shri Purohit Swami & Puran Singh
Large Format Paperback 7" x 10" 360 pages.

THE BOOK OF AMIR KHUSRAU
Translation & Introduction Paul Smith
Large Format Paperback 7" x 10" 441 pages

THE BOOK OF YUNUS EMRE
Translation & Introduction Paul Smith
Large Format Paperback 7" x 10" 253 pages

THE BOOK OF BABA TAHIR ORYAN
Translation & Introduction Paul Smith
Large Format Paperback 7" x 10" 187 pages

THE BOOK OF GHALIB
Translation & Introduction Paul Smith
Large Format Paperback 7" x 10" 194 pages

THE *RUBA'I* (QUATRAIN) IN SUFI POETRY
An Anthology
Translation & Introduction Paul Smith
Large Format Paperback 7" x 10" 450 pages

THE BOOK OF AL-MA'ARRI
Translation & Introduction Paul Smith
Large Format Paperback 7" x 10" 172 pages

THE BOOK OF ANVARI
Translation & Introduction Paul Smith
Large Format Paperback 7" x 10" 168 pages

THE BOOK OF KAMAL AL-DIN ISFAHANI
Translation & Introduction Paul Smith
Large Format Paperback 7" x 10" 170 pages

THE BOOK OF ABDUL-QADER BEDIL
Translation & Introduction Paul Smith
Large Format Paperback 7" x 10" 173 pages

THE BOOK OF BABA AFDAL KASHINI
Translation & Introduction Paul Smith
Large Format Paperback 7" x 10" 173 pages

THE BOOK OF ANSARI
Translation & Introduction Paul Smith
Large Format Paperback 7" x 10" 236 pages

~Introduction to Sufi Poets Series~

Life & Poems of the following Sufi poets, Translations & Introductions: Paul Smith

'AISHAH Al-BA'UNIYAH, AMIR KHUSRAU, ANSARI, ANVARI, AL-MA'ARRI, 'ATTAR, ABU SA'ID, AUHAD UD-DIN, BABA FARID, BABA AZFAL, BABA TAHIR, BEDIL, BULLEH SHAH, DARA SHIKOH, GHALIB, HAFIZ, IBN 'ARABI, IBN YAMIN, IBN AL-FARID, IQBAL, INAYAT KHAN, 'IRAQI, JAHAN KHATUN, JAMI, KAMAL AD-DIN, KABIR, KHAQANI, KHAYYAM, LALLA DED, MAKHFI, MANSUR HALLAJ, MU'IN UD-DIN CHISHTI, NAZIR AKBARABADI, NESIMI, NIZAMI, OBEYD ZAKANI, RAHMAN BABA, RUMI, SANA'I, SADI, SARMAD, SHABISTARI, SHAH LATIF, SHAH NI'MAT'ULLAH, SULTAN BAHU, YUNUS EMRE, EARLY ARABIC SUFI POETS, EARLY PERSIAN SUFI POETS, URDU SUFI POETS, TURKISH SUFI POETS, AFGHAN SUFI POETS 90 pages each.

POETRY

THE MASTER, THE MUSE & THE POET
An Autobiography in Poetry
by Paul Smith. 654 Pages.

~A BIRD IN HIS HAND~
POEMS FOR AVATAR MEHER BABA
by Paul Smith. 424 pages.

PUNE: THE CITY OF GOD
(A Spiritual Guidebook to the New Bethlehem)
Poems & Photographs in Praise of Avatar Meher Baba
by Paul Smith. 159 pages.

COMPASSIONATE ROSE
Recent *Ghazals* for Avatar Meher Baba
by Paul Smith. 88 pages.

~THE ULTIMATE PIRATE~
(and the Shanghai of Imagination)
A FABLE by Paul Smith. 157 pages.

+THE CROSS OF GOD+
A Poem in the *Masnavi* Form
by Paul Smith (7 x 10 inches)

RUBA'IYAT ~ of ~ PAUL SMITH
Pages 236.

SONG OF SHINING WONDER
& OTHER *MASNAVI* POEMS
Paul Smith. Pages 171.

~TEAMAKER'S *DIVAN*... *GHAZALS*~
Paul Smith. Pages 390.

CRADLE MOUNTAIN
Paul Smith... Illustrations – John Adam.
(7x10 inches) Second Edition.

~BELOVED & LOVER~
Ghazals by Paul Smith... inspired by Meher Baba
Pages 410.

POEMS INSPIRED BY 'GOD SPEAKS' BY MEHER BABA
Paul Smith... Pages 168.

MEHER BABA'S SECLUSION HILL
Poems & Photographs by Paul Smith
"7 x 10" 120 pages.

~DIVAN~ *Ghazals*... 1974 - 2014
Paul Smith. Pages 740

A BOOK OF QUATRAINS FOR THE ONE
by Paul Smith
Large Format 7" x 10" 511 pages.

FICTION

THE FIRST MYSTERY
A Novel of the Road…
by Paul Smith. 541 pages. Large Format Edition 589 pages

~THE HEALER AND THE EMPEROR~
A Historical Novel Based on a True Story
by Paul Smith Pages 149.

>>>GOING<<<BACK…
A Novel by Paul Smith. 164 pages.

THE GREATEST GAME
A Romantic Comedy Adventure With A Kick!
by Paul Smith 187 pages.

GOLF IS MURDER!
A Miles Driver Golfing Mystery
by Paul Smith. 176 pages.

THE ZEN-GOLF MURDER!
A Miles Driver Golfing Mystery
by Paul Smith 146 pages.

~RIANA~ A Novel
by Paul Smith 154 pages.

CHILDREN'S FICTION

PAN OF THE NEVER-NEVER
by Paul Smith 167 pages.

~HAFIZ~
The Ugly Little Boy who became a Great Poet
by Paul Smith 195 pages.

SCREENPLAYS

>>>GOING<<<BACK...
A Movie of War & Peace Based on a True Story...
Screenplay by Paul Smith

HAFIZ OF SHIRAZ
The Life, Poetry and Times of the Immortal Persian Poet.
A Screenplay by Paul Smith

LAYLA & MAJNUN BY NIZAMI
A Screenplay by Paul Smith

PAN OF THE NEVER-NEVER...
A Screenplay by Paul Smith

THE GREATEST GAME
A Romantic Comedy Adventure With A Kick!
A Screenplay
by Paul Smith

GOLF IS MURDER!
Screenplay
by Paul Smith

THE HEALER & THE EMPEROR
A True Story... Screenplay
by Paul Smith

THE * KISS ... A Screen-Play
by Paul Smith

THE ZEN-GOLF MURDER!
A Screenplay by Paul Smith

TELEVISION

HAFIZ OF SHIRAZ:
A Television Series
by Paul Smith

THE FIRST MYSTERY
A Television Series For The New Humanity
by Paul Smith

THE MARK: The Australian Game
A Thirteen-Part Doco-Drama for Television
by Paul Smith

PLAYS, MUSICALS

HAFIZ: THE MUSICAL DRAMA
by Paul Smith

THE SINGER OF SHIRAZ
A Radio Musical-Drama on the Life of Persia's Immortal Poet,
Hafiz of Shiraz by Paul Smith

MEMOIR

SLIPPING THROUGH THE CRACKS
A Memoir by Ron Roberts 186 pages

ART

MY DOGS
From the Sketchbooks of Gus Cohen. 8" x 10" 224 pages

A BRIDGE TO THE MASTER… MEHER BABA
Paintings & Drawings, Poems & Essays
by Oswald Hall
Edited & Introduction by Paul Smith   8" x 10" 337 pages.

MY VIEW
From the Sketchbooks of Gus Cohen,
Barkers Creek Castlemaine   8" x 10" 210 pages.

THE ART OF KEVIN SMITH
Paintings & Drawings, Sculpture, Furniture,
Mirrors, Boxes & Photographs
8" x 10" 337 pages full colour

> "To penetrate into the essence of all being and significance
> and to release the fragrance of that inner attainment
> for the guidance and benefit of others, by expressing
> in the world of forms, truth, love, purity and beauty…
> this is the only game which has any intrinsic and absolute
> worth. All other, happenings, incidents and attainments can,
> in themselves, have no lasting importance."
> Meher Baba